INTO THE
WOODS

Families Making
ART IN NATURE

Sue Fierston

SWINGING BRIDGE PRESS

WASHINGTON, D.C.

Let the beauty you love be what you do.

RUMI

CONTENTS

INTRODUCTION

TAKE A BREATH AND WALK INTO THE WOODS.

I encourage your family to use this book to rediscover the beauty and solace of the outdoors, to make art, and to enjoy the changing light and weather of the seasons.

You will find original meditative games in Section One, such as *The Eight Treasures*, that cultivate calm in the outdoors.

In Sections Two and Three, you'll find chapters on hand-printing leaves and fish, on contour drawing and painting, and on close observation in nature. Each chapter integrates the senses, combining direct observation of nature with touching and listening to the natural world.

Headnotes at the start of each chapter help you find the best activity for your family based on the ages of your children and the season. Many of the ideas, including Chapter 9's *Watercolor Printed Leaves*, can be put into practice by kids on their own. The chapters are independent of one another, so you can experiment with them in any order.

A list of supplies also starts off each activity, although the art supplies you will need are few and you may have many of them at home. A list of art suppliers and selected links and sources appear at the end of the book.

I hope you can use your art, your prints, and maybe your own practical ideas to create something beautiful and unusual, your family's own interpretation of these times.

fiustan
Yos. Falls

INTO NATURE

M EDITATIVE GAMES INVOKE PEACE AND CALM IN EVERYONE.

These five chapters are meant especially for families and groups of mixed ages.

Use the games in **Chapters 1** through **5** as bridges between indoors and outdoors or lively play and quieter times. To get started, all you need to do is walk out your front door.

Take time to debrief kids with the questions at the end of each game and they will surprise you with their thoughts.

CHAPTER 1

THE EIGHT TREASURES

SITTING WITH STILLNESS

STARTING

Age 8, works for younger children as a speaking game

BEST IN

Spring, to hear birds and to see the world wake up from winter's snow or rain

Summer, to watch clouds and the brilliant light

Fall, to notice the changing colors of grasses and leaves and the calls of birds in migration

Winter, to compare animal tracks in snow, patterns of tree branches, or to notice "what is different" at this season

WHERE

Outdoors sitting on grass, a curb, a bench; on a covered porch during the winter

TIME

Up to 45 minutes, easily shortened for younger children

THE EIGHT TREASURES CREATES MEDITATIVE CALM IN CHILDREN. It shows them how to become comfortable with stillness by breathing peacefully and observing the natural world around them.

As we look closely at nature's complexity, our sensitivity to other natural cues— a breeze on our skin, the scent of pine cones and crushed grass, the sounds of birds and the surf— connects us to the natural world. Nature's patterns and living systems can inspire designs in engineering or metaphors in poetry. This *biophilia,* or human-nature connection, is at the heart of the movement to include the arts in today's Science, Technology, Engineering, Mathematics school curriculum, making the familiar STEM into STEAM.

Eight questions may seem like seven too many when you're out with lively kids on a beautiful day! Yet, the very acts of breathing slowly and looking thoughtfully at a natural scene is calming and is a life skill worth learning. Everyone will become more peaceful by the end of the game, whether you play the entire game or decide to shorten it. Encourage kids to draw answers to the questions, if they choose.

In **Chapters 3** and **4,** you will find several more games that encourage meditative play including **Zen Camera, Recipe for a (Zen) Garden and Don't Eat That Raisin...Yet.**

You need

A copy of the Eight Treasures to read aloud

The children need

A pencil and hard-backed notebook or sketchbook at least 6 by 8 inches for each child.

OR A clipboard with loose paper, or a book with a paper clip to hold loose sheets works, too.

Folded towel or folded newspaper inside a trash bag for sitting on wet grass.

. . .

Let's start

1 Yoga breathing. The adult leads this breathing exercise with the children:

• While standing, stretch your hands over your head, reach for the stars, and take a slow, deep breath.

• Reach up to the sky again. Take another deep breath. As you breathe out, let your head fall to your chest and hands fall to your sides.

• Repeat one more time.

• The children sit down. *Tell them:* You have plenty of time to answer each question. I'll let you know when we're getting ready to move on to the next one.

2 Children sit at arm's length outside on the grass, in the sand at the beach, or at a picnic table. They have a pencil and a notebook to write in, but younger kids or kids who have difficulty writing can answer aloud.

• Simpler questions for younger children appear in parentheses.

• *Allow kids at least five minutes* to write or draw the answer to each question. If they take longer than five minutes to answer, that's great! *There is no rush to finish.* The peaceful pause between questions is part of this nature game.

• When kids start to giggle or get restless, simply say, "You'll feel calmer if you take a deep breath." Then take one yourself and continue.

Yosemite meadow grasses in morning light

THE EIGHT TREASURES

1 Look at something for five minutes.

2 What do you hear? Turn your head from side to side to hear differently. What is being communicated by what you hear?

(*For younger children,* be specific: What are the birds saying to each other? or Why are the waves crashing so loudly?)

7

3 Find beauty in an unexpected place. Draw or write about what you see.

4 Find two things, next to each other, that contrast in color. What are they? Draw them or write about them in a sentence or two.

Find two *more* things, next to each other, that contrast in size. What are they? Draw them or write about them in a sentence or two.

5 Find five signs of the approach of cooler (warmer) weather.

6 A treasure for you! Make an observation or write down a thought of your choice about what we are doing right now.

7 Select something to smell. Choose three words to describe the smell. There's no need to pick the flower, pine cone or bark, simply smell it.

8 What is the most important part of our natural world?

(*For younger children:* When I went outside today, I noticed...)

Debriefing the Eight Treasures is fascinating. Often children simply want to lay quietly on the grass at the end, looking off into the trees or up into the sky. Let them!

Ask the kids

• *What did you discover ?* Did you want the treasures not to end?

• *Which treasure was your favorite?* Why?

• *Talk with the kids about their answers.* Notice who decided to draw answers and who chose to write.

VARIATIONS

Try the Eight Treasures at different times of day or in different seasons.

Choose a favorite treasure and ask your kids about it as you travel together through a day or week.

Incorporate the three deep breaths at other times to invoke calm.

CHAPTER 2

ZEN CAMERA: WHAT DO OTHER PEOPLE SEE?

STARTING AT age 6 and anyone, including mixed child/adult pairs, can play

BEST IN Summer, Spring, Fall, any time the weather is fine for playing outside

WHERE playing outside builds most trust

TIME 30 minutes, can be shortened or lengthened easily

A SILENT GAME OF CLOSE OBSERVATION and trust-building, Zen Camera is played in pairs, outside. One person is the photographer (with eyes open) and the other a camera (blindfolded). Zen Camera builds trust between the pair, because the photographer must lead the blindfolded camera carefully over open ground to a spot to "take a picture."

Mixed-age pairs and child/adult pairs give extra power and responsibility to the younger member of the pair, as it is rare for a younger child to have the opportunity to take charge of an adult or older sibling.

Let's start

Each pair is made up of a photographer and a camera. After three "pictures," the photographer and camera switch roles. Feel free to modify the total number of pictures taken depending on the ages of the players.

You need a scarf or towel for each pair to use as a blindfold. Kids tend to peek, even when you ask them to squeeze their eyes shut.

1 The camera closes her eyes.

2 The photographer carefully leads the camera
to the place where they will take the picture.

3 The photographer moves the body of the camera and tilts her head until it is pointing at the sight the photographer wants the camera to see.

4 The photographer squeezes the shoulder of the camera when the picture is set up, and removes the blindfold. The camera opens her eyes. Without speaking, the camera looks at the scene or object until the photographer squeezes the camera's shoulder again.

5 The camera puts the blindfold back on and the photographer leads the camera silently to the location for the next picture.

Zen Camera may be played silently, but players will be bursting to talk by the end of it. Particularly, they will want to know if their partner saw or "took a picture" of what they intended him or her to see. Many times, the person playing the camera focuses on something completely different from what the photographer intended; occasionally, the camera sees nothing of interest at all when they open their eyes!

Ask

• *How did it go?* Did the cameras see what the photographers wanted them to see? If not, what got in the way?

• *Did the camera see something the photographer didn't notice?*

• *How did it feel to be a camera?* A photographer? Did one role fit better than the other? Was one more fun? Why?

• *What if our own cameras were alive* and took only the pictures they liked?

VARIATION

Paint or draw what you saw as the camera. You will find drawing and painting activities in **Chapter 6 Take Line for a Walk** and **Ch. 7 Take Color for a Walk.**

CHAPTER 3

THE SENSE OF TOUCH: RECIPE FOR A (ZEN) GARDEN

STARTING AT age 6

BEST IN any season, great for a rainy day inside

WHERE collect materials outside or inside on a rainy day, build the Zen garden at any table

TIME 30 minutes, easily shortened or lengthened

K IDS, PARTICULARLY THOSE BETWEEN AGES 7 AND 10, love to create tiny imaginary worlds. Here they build their own Zen gardens on a small scale, collecting materials outside and arranging them in a tray on a bed of white sand. Calming sensory play, in particular smoothing the sand in the tray, and running fingers over the patterns of the objects creates the calm atmosphere. See the story in this chapter for more information on Japanese Zen gardens including Ryoan-ji, the famous Kyoto Zen rock garden.

Traditional Zen rock gardens are Japanese landscapes designed to encourage meditation. Rocks, trees and shrubs are selected by the landscape designer to evoke memories and associations, and their placement, in beds of moss or white gravel, is careful and deliberate. Often the gravel is raked in patterns to evoke wave patterns in water. Some gardens include a bell or gong to ring when entering.

You need

Clean white sand (feels best in the hand); clean, dry builder's sand or beach sand will work

Bag for objects collected by children on a nature walk

Tray or box with sides up to 4 inches high (a shoe box top or a left-over box from the garden center works well) to be the garden and contain the sand. A container the size of a sheet of paper or a bit larger is good to start with; younger children will find it easier to work with a larger tray, older kids can manage a small one.

fork or spoon

ruler or smooth stick

bell, gong, iPhone with birdsong or spoon that can be tapped on an empty glass

Let's start

The nature walk can be as organized or as free as you like. You can find items for the tiny Zen garden anywhere, in your backyard, on a hike, in the house on a rainy day. Your only constraint is that the items kids collect must fit on the tray! Here are a few collecting ideas:

- Collect anything that catches your eye as a record of the day.

- Look for things that have different textures: smooth stones, rough bark, spiky seashells.

- Collect only one type of thing, say stones, but as many different shapes, colors and sizes as you can find.

- Choose objects of only one color: black seeds, black rocks, black sticks.

- Look for items of different sizes: big shells, small dried crabs, tiny pieces of coral.

- If you're collecting indoors on a rainy day, use these same ideas to collect whatever you have in the house: nails, buttons, spools of thread, yarn, crayons, tiny colorful plastic building blocks.

Building the garden

1 Take a nature walk and collect objects for your garden

2 Pour white sand into the tray to a depth of at least an inch. Deeper sand allows you to partially bury an object in the sand, creating atmosphere and mystery

3 Smooth sand so it lays evenly in the tray using the ruler or a stick

4 Create patterns on the sand by drawing in it with the fork, a finger or a stick

5 Arrange items on the sand. Younger children can arrange in patterns, older ones may want to experiment with grouping similar objects together. Rearrange items as you wish.

Ask the kids

- *Tell me about your garden,* its shapes, its objects.

- *What made you choose these things?*

- *Where should we look first?* Why?

- *Show me your favorite path* through the garden.

VARIATIONS

- Experiment with different types of sand, coarse verses fine, or colored sand

• Add the sense of sound by playing birdsong as children design their gardens

• Include a tiny bell for atmosphere or make a bell by tapping a spoon on a glass partly filled with water

• If you have a large tray, several kids can work together to design the garden

GOOD TO KNOW

Zen rock gardens

At the Temple of the Peaceful Dragon in Kyoto, Japan, 15 large and small rocks sit in clusters on a bed of raked white sand. Ryoan-ji, as it is known, has become the most famous Zen rock garden in the world since it was built in the 1400s. From a distance, the rocks resemble islands in a peaceful sea.

Ryoan-ji raked stone garden (photo: Flavio on Flickr, 2.0 generic CC BY 2.0)

Other cultures link the word "garden" to flowering plants, trees and color. Zen rock gardens typically have little color and visitors focus and meditate on the shape of the rocks and on the precise patterns of the raked sand surrounding them.

Our fascination with these gardens may come from their very spareness, and some artists suggest that they be called "Zen rock sculptures" instead.

CHAPTER 4

DON'T EAT THAT RAISIN...YET

STARTING AT age 8

BEST IN a shady spot during summer months or indoors on a rainy or cold day

WHERE sitting indoors or outside

TIME 5 to 10 minutes

FOCUS ATTENTION ON THE SENSE OF TASTE by eating one raisin…very slowly. If you substitute a cookie the first time you play, the temptation to eat it right away may be overwhelming for a child. Start with the somewhat dull raisin and then, depending on the willpower of you and the kids, try other foods on other days.

This game also encourages kids to see familiar things with fresh eyes.

You need

One raisin per child and one for you

Let's start

Each step should last at least 30 seconds, longer if possible.

1 Tell children that they are travelers from Mars and know nothing about the object you are about to give them. That means a person from Mars wouldn't even know a raisin was a food.

2 Put a raisin in the palm of each child.

3 Hold the raisin in the palm of your hand. Remind the kids that they have never seen a raisin before. Ask them: Is it heavy?

(Holding up to an ear) Does it make sound? What if you sang to it?

(In your hand) What if you shook it?

4 Pick up the raisin. Look at it up close, at the wrinkles and fissures that make up its skin. Smell the raisin.

5 Bring the raisin up to your lips. Does it feel hot or cold against your skin?

6 Touch the raisin with your tongue. Does it have a flavor?

7 Take a tiny bite and chew. Can you taste the flavor? Is it what you expected?

8 Put the whole raisin in your mouth and let it sit there, without chewing, as long as you can. What happens in your mouth? How do you feel?

9 How slowly can you chew this tiny raisin? What is its flavor? How does the flavor change as you chew?

10 Can you feel the raisin as it moves down your throat to your stomach?

Surprise reigns at the end of **Don't Eat That Raisin...Yet**— all players are surprised by how fascinating a raisin has become. The very slowness of the game brings on the fascination. When you play it with other foods, the surprise won't be as acute, but the fascination will still be there.

VARIATIONS

• *Seeing food as an alien* from another planet is a fun way to reframe eating. Try other foods from the dull, such as celery, to the exciting, such as mango.

• If playing this game with two children or more, *give each child a different food* and compare answers at the end of the game.

• *Play this game out in nature.* Examine a pine cone, a flower, a stone...anything that you can touch and hold. You can ask kids to imagine how the object would taste, and substitute questions that prompt the other senses such as, "Can I make music with these three stones?"

CHAPTER 5

SLIP ON YOUR SHOES AND STEP OUTSIDE

AND CREATE SCULPTURES FROM NATURE

W HEN THE TIME ISN'T RIGHT for an organized game, you might scoop up the family and go out for a walk. Try these five quick ideas to make the walk lively:

• *Stop and look at something every 10 steps,* every block, or every 10 houses. Take turns being the person who chooses what to look at.

• *Take a tip from the Ministry of Silly Walks* and hop, leap or dance down the street in the silliest, most leg-lifting way possible.

• *Create a scavenger hunt.* List five objects to search for along the way such as a robin, a fire escape, a person wearing a backpack, something orange, a flower growing in an unexpected place.

. . .

• *Take a silent walk* with a leader. The leader, an adult or child, points at fascinating, unusual or funny things along the way. Everyone tries to keep from talking until the end of the walk, which will be difficult and part of the fun. On the return trip, switch leaders.

• *Look for the things you love.* They don't even have to be from nature. If your family loves airplanes, count contrails in the sky and if your kids love counting dogs wearing coats, do that. What's most important is that you enjoy your time in the fresh air.

GOOD TO KNOW: SCULPTURES FROM NATURE

We are all collectors at heart. Some kids collect coins and others collect baseball cards. And, when you go outside you can collect rocks and flower petals, snowballs and mud to make your own sculptures. British artist Andy Goldsworthy does just that, leaving the natural sculptures he makes from these objects to weather and erode, reflecting nature and its constant growth, movement and change.

Andy Goldsworthy's stone cone sculpture at the Frank Lloyd Wright house, Kentuck Knob, in Pennsylvania (Photo: Scott Robinson on flickr CC BY 2.0)

On a walk or in your yard try

- *collecting* leaves, sticks, stones, any natural items that you can collect multiples of
- *arranging* them in a group pattern
- or working alone, create your own pattern
- *photographing* your sculpture when you finish, and
- *returning* one day, one week and one month later, documenting what you see with photos or in your sketchbook from **Chapter 8**

OBSERVING NATURE

W E ALL WANT TO RECORD WHAT WE SEE.

Kids from age eight and up, with adult help, will get the most out of these chapters. Children 12 and older can draw, paint, and create their own sketchbooks independently.

Start a family sketchbook and fill it with color! **Chapter 6** teaches the meditative art of contour drawing and **Chapter 7** reveals the secrets behind color choice and emotional color. **Chapter 8** brings these ideas together, showing kids and families how to keep sketchbooks and become citizen scientists.

CHAPTER 6

TAKE A LINE FOR A WALK:
CONTOUR DRAWING

THE SLOWER YOU GO, THE BETTER THE DRAWING

Daffodil and Bluebell, Watercolor and ink
contour drawing on paper, 12 x 14 inches

BEST IN

Any season, also good for days when you cannot go outside

STARTING

Age 8 with adult help, age 11 and up alone

WHERE

Outside or inside

TIME

Five minutes for the first drawing

M OST PEOPLE FIND CONTOUR DRAWING MEDITATIVE AND PEACEFUL...ONCE THEY GET STARTED. Betty Edwards, in *Drawing on the Right Side of the Brain*, sees drawing as a skill that anyone can learn, just as we all learn to read. "Learning to draw is more than learning the skill itself," she says, "... by learning to draw you are learning to see in the special way used by artists."

But, many adults find it hard to begin. It can be tough to put aside years of thinking that you can't draw to give one more thought to the idea that you can.

This kid-tested method will also show children how to create accurate drawings. Around age nine, children are especially interested in drawing things "how they look" because, as they enter adolescence, they are learning how to see accurately.

As you learn to draw, you'll actually feel a physical change in your hand as you start drawing what you really see: your family, a vacation view, a leaf.

Remind everyone to take several deep breaths both before starting to draw and at any time while drawing when you find yourself thinking "I can't do this" or "This is too difficult." You'll find that the drawing problem solves itself if you stop for a minute and breathe.

CONTOUR DRAWING: HAND

Contour drawing is unique among drawing techniques because this style of drawing— in a continuous line, without stopping— creates a meditative peace in an artist. In contour drawing you keep your pencil line going and save your erasing until the end. Kids and adults often use contour drawing to create extremely realistic and expressive drawings.

The key is to draw slowly. Tell yourself and your kids: *The slower you go, the better the drawing.*

Let's start by drawing something you always have at hand: your hand. Hands are expressive, unique and, if you know the manual alphabet for the deaf, you can form a letter of the alphabet with your fingers and draw that! Laura Rankin's *Handmade Alphabet* uses Rankin's colored contour drawings of hands to display the correct position for each letter of the manual alphabet.

Kids love to draw their own hand held in the shape of an initial. Tell the kids (and yourself!) "Put your other hand (the non-drawing one) in any position that you can hold for five minutes."

Some kids say, "Why can't I just trace my hand? It fits right on the paper!" The truth is, they can. But they can use contour drawing to draw larger things, like ferris wheels, dogs, or mountains, and they can't trace them!

Supplies

You can use any pencil and copy paper for these drawings. You'll find compressed charcoal and a spiral-bound sketchbook at any art supply store or online at Dick Blick or Amazon. Spiral-bound sketchbooks are great because they lay flat when opened, which is especially good for the left-handed among us.

You need

Pencil

Paper

Compressed charcoal, gives dark marks, great for creating shadows

Sketchbook, an easy way to organize and keep track of drawings. A useful size is 8 x 10 inches, not too big and easy to fit into a backpack.

NO eraser, at least at first

Especially if this is your child's (or your own) very first drawing, everyone should be as relaxed as possible. Deep breathing calms the mind and it will help a child create their first contour drawing, quieting that left side of the brain that will be tempting them to draw a smiley face and move on!

So say this first:

Let's do some deep breathing! Let your head fall to your chest and your hands fall to your sides. Even if you feel silly, take two more deep breaths in the same way.

Let's start

1 Take out a sheet of paper and pencil.

2 Place the non-drawing hand in one position for five minutes.

3 Warm up by simply *looking* at the contours, the outline, of this hand, from wrist to thumb to fingers, to wrist again.

If you're holding that hand in a position in which you can't see a finger (or two), don't worry. You should draw what you see, even if it feels odd to draw a hand with fewer than the usual five fingers.

If you need to add details to the drawing after you have done the contour itself, you can add them at the end.

4 Begin drawing at the wrist. Slowly move your eyes up the edge of your hand, beginning at your wrist. Let your pencil begin drawing at the same time, slowly making a continuous line as your eye travels up the edge of the hand.

Don't lift the pencil from the paper. If you need to reverse course to connect lines, that's ok, but if you make an outright mistake, just keep drawing. Tell yourself you can erase and fix the problem at the end.

5 When you feel impatient or stuck, take a deep breath. The drawing problem will seem to solve itself. Kids often show impatience by giggling and poking a neighbor. The solution is the same: take a deep breath.

6 When you have finished drawing the contour of your hand, go back in and add details. Fingernails, watches, wrinkles are all things to add after after you've finished drawing the main contours.

7 The slower you go, the better the drawing. That said, your first drawing will be good, but it won't be your best. No one learns to read by starting with Shakespeare, and learning to draw is the same: it starts with hands and progresses to trees and mountain ranges and portraits.

• *If a child finishes in one minute,* he or she has gone too quickly. Best to start again after taking a few more deep breaths.

• *Conversely, if a person is still drawing after five minutes,* I don't stop them. Some children (and adults) get lost in the act of contour drawing from their first try. I wait until they are finished.

8 After you finish, you can go back in and add details, such as a ring or watch, to your drawing. Check to see if you have drawn each fingernail as a unique shape, it is too easy and quick to draw a generic "fingernail shape." If you look closely at your fingertips, you will see that each fingernail has a unique shape and size.

9 Sign and date your work, and congratulations!
You have completed your first contour drawing.

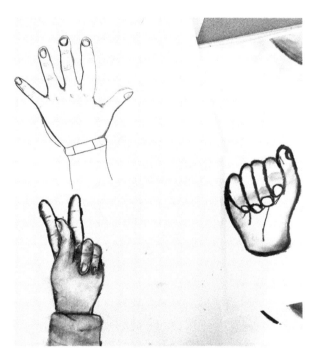

Student drawings, manual alphabet, letters K and A using compressed charcoal on copy paper.

CONTOUR DRAWING: MORE COMPLEXITY

Take it up a level and have your family draw a shoe, a leaf, or a bumpy gourd from the farmers' market. Allow kids up to 15 minutes to complete this drawing, depending on the complexity of the object they've chosen.

Some children will be ready to draw the whole world at this stage, but ask them to slow down. This is their chance to master contour drawing and really become an expert.

This drawing of the maple leaf took me about 15 minutes and the watercolor paint that I added took another 10 minutes.

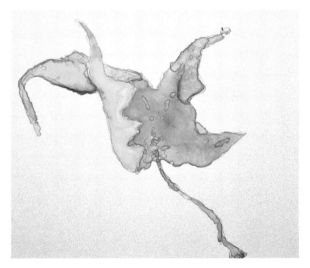

Maple leaf in fall, watercolor on Yupo, 6 x 6 inches

Let's start

1 Arrange the shoe or other object in a position that pleases you. Remember, shoes don't have to rest on their soles—in fact, they often have patterns on their soles that are fascinating to draw.

2 Take out a sheet of paper and pencil.

3 Remind the kids to take three deep breaths. They should tell themselves "I can do this!"

With a group of kids, you might also ask: *What do you need to do to make a good drawing?*

The answer is to go slow, and take a deep breath when they feel stuck with the drawing. Although the deep breath seems as if it would interrupt the flow, it actually sets the stage for a successful drawing by calming that impatient, doubting side of the brain, the left side.

4 Begin drawing at a place that looks simple. On a shoe, that might be the long contour of the sole. On a gourd, that may be the smooth curve on the stem handle.

Slowly move your eyes over the contours of your object, moving your eyes back and forth between the paper and your hand. Try to move the pencil in one continuous line. If you make a mistake, just keep drawing, don't stop to erase.

5 When you feel impatient or stuck, take another deep breath. The drawing problem will seem to solve itself.

6 The slower you go, the better the drawing.

7 Go back in and add details, such as shoelaces or

the bumps on a gourd after you have finished the overall contour drawing. Go back into the drawing and erase any lines you can't live with.

8 Sign and date your work, well done!

CONTOUR DRAWING: ADDING SHADOWS

Kids love to create the illusion of 3D by using compressed charcoal or a dark pencil to color in the darkest dark of shadows. Shadows are often much darker than we realize, and they add illusion and mystery to a drawing. The contour drawings of hands show shading with compressed charcoal.

Let's start

1 Begin with a contour drawing that is complete.

2 Imagine the direction that sunlight is coming from, either actually what you saw or by simply choosing an upper right or left corner. With pencil, I often lightly draw a tiny sun right on the drawing to remind myself of the direction of the light.

3 The brightest spots in the drawing are closest to the light.

4 The darkest spots are furthest away from the light, in the opposite corner of the drawing or blocked from direct light. Think of shadows under the hand, under rocks, under trees.

5 Using compressed charcoal or the side of your pencil, shade those areas that are furthest away from the light. Darken shadows by increasing the pressure on your pencil or charcoal.

Encourage yourself to make them very dark! Most people have a light hand when adding shadows, but the darker you make them, the more the drawing will pop.

VARIATIONS

Draw with a colored pencil or crayon

Contour drawing using a colored pencil or crayon creates a fun, energetic mood no matter what the subject is. Try drawing the hand in different positions using different colors, such as bright orange and navy blue, or several shades of green, to create drawings with extra pizzaz. For more about color combinations, see **Chapter 7.**

Draw with a fat tip or fine tip marker

The thickness of a line, called line weight, gives personality to a drawing. To create the illusion of distance in a drawing, experiment with drawing close-up objects with a thick point jumbo marker and far away objects with a fine tip marker. Without adding much color, the drawing will take on a sense of depth.

*Grocery bag contour drawing, Marblehead
Harbor at Dusk, jumbo marker and watercolor,
12 x 6 inches.*

Try a colored surface

A tan grocery bag is a wonderful surface for drawing on,

and it's what I used in the sketch of the sailboat. The paper's rough surface grabs the pencil and the color makes it easy to add highlights and shadows to the composition. Grocery store bags are a great source for this brown kraft paper, but these bags are hard to flatten perfectly and leave behind creases when you try.

You can also find kraft paper bound into sketchbooks for more formal (and flat) drawings.

We are so accustomed to drawing on white paper that any dark paper—black, blue, brown, red—is fun to experiment with. Try drawing with white chalk on black paper!

CHAPTER 7

TAKE COLOR FOR A WALK: WATERCOLORS

ADD REALISTIC (OR PLAYFUL) COLOR TO YOUR DRAWINGS

Marblehead Harbor, 5 AM. Ink and watercolor on paper, 10" x 8"

E VERYONE HAS A FAVORITE COLOR and, because of that, these color activities are for everyone, from young children to the oldest family member.

Try them as easy entertainment when the family is gathered or as a playful way to break the ice. Each activity takes between 20 and 30 minutes as written, but these activities can be expanded or shortened to fill the time you have.

We tell stories through color as we choose our clothing, flowering plants, and our art. Without realizing it, we use color to tell stories that reflect the seasons or our feelings. You and your family can create sketchbooks in **Chapter 8** and make nature prints in **Chapters 9, 10** and **11** using your unique color ideas from this chapter.

Your family likely has the supplies on hand—crayons, simple watercolors, a paintbrush, copy paper—to start playing with color. These supplies are all you need for the three color activities in this chapter. Kids can share a water-color set or large box of crayons, but they each will want their own water brush!

You can buy other suggested supplies online at Dick Blick or on Amazon.

SUGGESTED SUPPLIES

Something to add color:

> **Watercolor crayons or pencils.** Caran d'Ache, Sargent, and Prismacolor are brands that have many choices of strong, saturated colors.

OR Regular wax crayons

OR A simple watercolor set such as Yarka or Reeves brand 12 color.

Something to paint with:

One round tip and one flat tip watercolor paintbrush Sizes #6, 8 or 10 and one large flat tip size 1 inch. The paintbrush that comes with an inexpensive paint box is a good start, but a slightly fancier brush will be more fun to use because it holds more paint. Each shape of brush makes a distinctly different mark.

OR Niji waterbrush, flat or pointed tip. A water brush is like a fountain pen: but, instead of ink, it holds a reservoir of water in its handle. This water drips out the tip of the brush when you squeeze the plastic handle. Kids love them.

Convenient for travel, water brushes tuck in your pocket and mean you don't need to carry a separate water bottle for painting. Along my travels, I have filled my water brush in anything from streams to water fountains!

Something to paint on:

Copy paper

OR a watercolor sketchbook (see **Chapter 8**)

Something to hold water:

Any small plastic container if you are using a

regular paintbrush. I have often used the cap from my water bottle to rinse my paintbrush in.

Something to mop it up:

Paper towels

USING WATERCOLOR CRAYONS OR PENCILS

Tuck three watercolor crayons in your pocket, grab a few water brushes and paper, and head out the door with your family. That's all it takes to start painting outside.

Watercolor crayons and pencils are simply made of paint hardened into sticks. You can use them dry as you would regular wax crayons, but their magic lies in using them wet.

Here are five ways to get started. You can try these techniques along with the kids and the fifth suggestion, the ribbon of color, is the most dramatic and fun.

Try

• Dipping the crayon in water, then drawing on paper. The crayon color will start out saturated and dark. As the crayon dries out, its color will become lighter.

• Wetting the paper with clear water, then drawing on the wet paper. Your marks will be dark, as the crayon races across the wet area. It will skid to a stop on dry paper.

• Wetting the paintbrush, rubbing it on the crayon, then painting on paper. This method produces smooth color washes and is good for filling in delicate contour drawings.

• Scribbling on dry paper, then painting the scribble with a wet paintbrush. The scribbles will turn to paint, leaving behind a few darker scribble marks.

• Creating a ribbon of color by wetting the large flat brush and coloring directly on it with two or three different watercolor crayons. The brush should be so wet that it drips. Then, paint with the brush and see the ribbon unfold!

DO YOU LOVE COLOR?

What's your own connection to color? Do you wear the same colors every day, or do you match your color choices to the season? Are there colors you love or just can't stand?

Find out your family's color preferences and let your kids play with color in the three sections below: **Emotional Color, Colors I like,** and **Seasonal Color.**

Emotional color • *30 minutes or roughly 5 minutes per emotion*

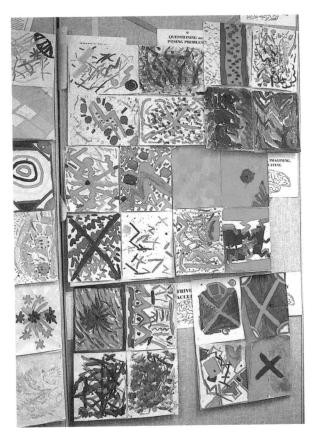

Emotional color: Anger painted using only symbolic color

This activity is great for everyone.

Even the youngest child will be able to match strong feelings, such as love and anger, to color. What to say to the youngest kids appears in parenthesis within the activity. Older kids will be able to interpret all the emotions including more subtle feelings such as envy or peacefulness.

You can include at least six different emotions in this lesson before the attention of children starts to fade. Use a new piece of paper for each emotion. The completed emotions, vivid with color, look wonderful displayed together on a wall.

Setting up the game

• Try these vivid emotions:

anger, joy, sadness, energy, envy, peacefulness

(For younger kids, try the first three emotions and add "fun" as the fourth.)

> • *Here's the tricky part: explain to the children that they should use lines, shapes and color* to fill the paper. They shouldn't draw smiley faces or hearts or tears or words or numbers. There is a deep connection between emotion and color, and drawing simple lines and shapes will let it emerge.
>
> (This is often easier for young children than for older ones because the young ones haven't yet learned the "smiley face" or "teardrop" symbols.)

• The parent or leader should read one emotion at a time, allowing at least five minutes between emotions for the kids to fill in their paper.

• After they are finished, kids should label the paper with the emotion and put it aside.

. . .

Let's start

• *Everyone start with yoga breathing to refresh and center the mind.*
It can seem like a whirlwind to channel emotional
extremes only five minutes apart!

The leader or parent should say:

*Stretch your hands into the air. Take a deep breath. Let your head
fall to your chest and hands fall by your sides.*

Repeat twice more.

• So everyone has a chance to feel each emotion before
they start to draw, *remind everyone to take a deep breath* and let
the emotion travel from their head…down past their
ear…down their shoulder…past their elbow…over their
wrist…and into their hand.

• *To start, choose a strong emotion* to imagine, such as anger
or joy.

• Remind the kids to *use the colors that are important to them,*
regardless of the colors other kids may choose.

• Tell them: *If you really love a certain color, use a lot of it* and
make it saturated and dark. If you like a color, but don't
love it, use less of it and paint lightly.

• *Leave at least five minutes for each emotion* and time at the
end to look over the paintings. Take time to wonder
about the colors people have in common and colors that
are unique to each person.

Ask

Children are often talkative after this activity. Many want to explain what they were thinking as they created their color interpretations.

Take time to listen and ask open-ended questions such as: *Which one of these was easy for you? Can you tell me what you were thinking about as you drew peacefulness?* Their answers may surprise you.

Colors I like / Colors I Don't Like • *20 minutes*

Everyone can answer the first question, but when have we really thought about the second one? Let your kids discover their color preferences and, once they know, they can choose color deliberately to make expressive paintings.

This activity works best with children over age 6. Each child needs two sheets of paper and crayons. Kids can also use water-color crayons and paint their answers to these two questions.

Let's start

• Give each child one sheet of paper. They should label it "Colors I Like."

• Using only lines and shapes (as in the Emotional Color activity), ask the child to fill in the first sheet **using ONLY colors they like.** If they don't like a color, even if other kids do, they shouldn't change. They should use only colors they like.

• If they really love a certain color, they should use a lot of it and make it saturated and dark. If they like a color, but don't love it, they should use less of it and color or paint lightly.

• Again, they shouldn't bother drawing rainbows, fancy cars, or balloons. This exercise is simply meant to show them their own color preferences.

• Some children say they love all the colors! They should go ahead and use them all. And, for **Colors I Don't Like,** they can leave a blank sheet of paper, which is a powerful statement.

Usually, though, a child does dislike some color. While drawing with the color over 10 minutes, many kids find, strangely enough, that they suddenly like it more!

Ask

When everyone is finished (and this usually takes 10 minutes), take time to look at the paintings. *Which colors do people have in common? Which colors are unique?*

If you have a culturally diverse group, or a group of many ages, you may find that there is no agreement on well-loved colors and it is fascinating to talk about why.

Repeat these steps substituting ***Colors I Don't Like.*** Change the instructions to reflect the idea of disliking certain colors, for example, say, "If you really dislike yellow, use a lot of it to express that feeling."

• • •

Seasonal color • *20 minutes*

Our emotions are linked to the seasons, too. Some of us feel energetic in winter, some in summer. Some find the oranges of fall energizing and others love the shocking yellows of the summer sun. Your family can record these preferences and create a journal of the seasons simply by using color as a tool to mark time. For example, you might say, "Let's draw today using only the colors of this season, the colors of winter ."

> • Yoga breathing helps too, as you channel each season and transcribe its colors onto paper. So, at the start of this activity, tell the kids: *Stretch your hands into the air. Take a deep breath. Let your head fall to your chest and hands fall by your sides.*

Then, before changing to the next season, remind everyone to take a deep breath and let the season travel from their head...down past their ear...down their shoulder...past their elbow...over their wrist...and into their hand.

You will need four sheets of paper per child (one for each season), and wax or watercolor crayons.

Let's start

• *Begin this activity* using the season you are currently in.

• Tell the children:

> *Using only lines and shapes,* fill the paper with color reflecting this season. Use the colors that are important to you, regardless of colors other people may choose.

If you really love a certain color, if it really reflects the colors you see at that season, use a lot of it and make it saturated and dark. If you like a color, but don't love it, use less of it and paint lightly.

Don't bother drawing objects.

• It is hard for kids not to draw snowflakes and beach umbrellas with this activity because they are so firmly fixed in our minds as symbols of a season. Encourage them to hang in there with this new idea and perhaps take a deep breath.

• *Leave at least five minutes for each season* and a few minutes more at the end to talk about the paintings. As before in the other color activities, take time to consider colors people have in common and colors that are unique.

GOOD TO KNOW

Color combinations create mood

Prisms reflect light as a rainbow, with colors arranged by wavelength: red, orange, yellow, green, blue, indigo and violet. Color wheels organize color in a circle to make it easy for artists to find and combine paint for different emotional effects.

What mood would you like to create?

• *Excitement and energy—use complementary color.* Colors opposite each other on a color wheel are complementary. If you use opposite colors, such as green and red, as the main colors in a painting, it will have extra vitality.

• *Peace and harmony—use analogous color.* Colors next to each other on the color wheel, such as green and blue, are called analogous colors. If you use only analogous color in a painting, you will create a calm mood. I think of these colors as the "friends" combination.

Sketchbook drawing, Yosemite National Park, ink and watercolor, 5 x 7 inches

Ask

Which combination do you like best?

Are you someone who likes the energetic style or do you like the "friends" style more?

Try

• Make a painting in one combination and then make the same painting in the other. It is hard to make the switch!

• Put them up on the wall side by side and talk with the kids about the different emotions that the colors bring up.

GOOD TO KNOW

Prisms and color wheels leave out black, white and gray. That means they don't show us a color we know so well, the color of our own skin.

Artist Byron Kim painted 10 x 8 inch paintings to match the skin tone of his family and friends, then organized the small paintings into a huge mural. This work, called *Synecdoche*, is in the collection of the National Gallery of Art in Washington, D.C. and measures 9 x 24 feet.

CHAPTER 8

TAKE A SKETCHBOOK FOR A WALK

STARTING

Age 6

BEST IN

Any time you and your family head out the front door for a walk, when you take a vacation, or when you are sitting at a favorite spot in your house, perhaps looking out the window.

WHERE

Outside or inside

TIME

Ten minutes or longer

*Mariposa Lily, Watercolor and ink on paper, 12
x 12 inches*

N OW THAT YOU AND YOUR FAMILY CAN DRAW AND PAINT
the world around you, you can keep track of your art
in a sketchbook. I use one that is small, no bigger than 12 x
12 inches, because this size fits easily in my bag.

My sketchbook collection goes back many years. When I
open an old sketchbook, I remember exactly how I felt and
what I was thinking when I drew the picture. I usually note
the time and sometimes write down a list of the sounds
around me. In many ways, the sketch brings the scene to life
better than a photo could, because I draw only what
catches my eye and leave the rest out.

In the sketch of the Mariposa lily, the stem that included an open flower caught my attention. I ignored every other stem of the lily and drew the stem I liked best.

If you and your family would like to learn to draw, see **Chapter 6**, and if you'd like to know more about water-color paints and choosing color, see **Chapter 7.**

1 How do I choose a sketchbook?

• **For kids 10 and older,** choose a sketchbook that fits easily in a backpack with paper that can take some water. Strathmore 400 spiral bound sketchbooks are inexpensive and include tough paper that can absorb wet paint without ripping.

For my own work, that means a Handbook sketchbook that measures 12 x 12 inches or 5 x 7 inches. This brand comes with a clear pocket inside the back cover of the book that is perfect for holding flat travel souvenirs such as maps or tickets or tiny flowers.

• **For younger children,** an 8 x 10 inch or larger sketchbook with spiral binding is easy to open, lays flat, and has plenty of surface area for drawing with crayons.

• Stapling sheets of copy paper together is an inexpensive way to make a sketchbook. If you try this, remember that thin copy paper works best with dry pencils and crayons, and it will wrinkle with wet paint.

These brands and other similar ones are available at local craft stores and online at Dick Blick and Amazon with prices ranging from $5 to $15.

. . .

2 Can any drawing, even a rough sketch, go into a sketchbook? Can I leave a drawing unfinished?

Your kids may include drawings of favorite animals, people or boats. They can draw comics or they can just play with color. Sketchbook drawings can be incomplete, ugly, or not perfect. They are a wonderful visual record of a child's growth and thoughts and, in a family sketchbook, a group record of your travels and family holidays.

3 What supplies do we need?

You and your family can simply take a walk with a few crayons and a sketchbook. Sometimes I go out to sketch with only a sketchbook and a pencil.

- To add color to the drawings, colored pencils and regular crayons will do the job. Many families keep a zipper lock bag of drawing supplies in the car or tucked by the front door so the supplies are easy to grab on the way outside.

- When I want to add paint to my drawings, I bring along a pocket-sized watercolor set and a water brush, too. I like to travel light when I'm out sketching and the water brush is lighter to carry than an extra water bottle.

- I often bring an aluminum camping stool or a few newspapers tucked into a plastic garbage bag to sit on.

Sketchbook painting supplies

For more detail on choosing these supplies, see **Chapter 7.**

Two or three watercolor crayons (which turn into watercolor paint when wet) or pencils or regular wax crayons

Small 12 color watercolor set

Water brush, flat or round tip. A water brush is like a fountain pen but, instead of ink, it holds a reservoir of water in its handle.

One paintbrush round tip size 8, or flat tip size 1 inch, if you don't bring a water brush

Water container, made of plastic, if you don't bring a water brush

Paper towel

Two sketchbooks, a blue-handled waterbrush, and two palettes of watercolor. The smaller palette at front was home-made with a rectangular mint tin and a plastic grid. I squeezed tube watercolors into each square of the grid.

Becoming a close observer

It's easy to fill up a sketchbook when we are away from home. But what can we put in a sketchbook when we are at home, perhaps walking to the same park day after day?

Slowing down to see and describe seasonal change is part of *phenology*, the study of nature's cycles. In this activity, you and your family return to a favorite place in your neighborhood over several days, weeks, or seasons and create a logbook of nature observations. Each child can record observations in his or her own sketchbook, or you can record family observations in one large sketchbook.

Take your time as you record the data. Add or subtract from the basic list as you wish, for example, your family might be counting deer or watching the opening flower buds of a magnolia tree.

You need

One sketchbook for each person, or one for the family and at least a pencil. Kids can make their own notes or an older child or parent can make notes for the group.

Let's start

1 Choose a welcoming spot in your yard or at a park or beneath a favorite tree. This should be a spot where everyone can sit comfortably for at least 15 minutes.

2 Take a few deep breaths, sit down, and observe the scene.

3 Open the sketchbook and record the time. Make note of the temperature or have everyone guess the temperature and look it up when you return home.

If it is autumn, the chirp of the male cricket is an excellent predictor of outside temperature. Only the male cricket chirps. Someone in the group will need a watch.

Count the number of chirps in 15 seconds. Add 37. The sum equals the rough temperature in degrees Fahrenheit. For a more accurate temperature, count the chirps of several different sounding crickets and average the results. Some crickets naturally chirp faster or slower than others, and averaging will give you the most accurate estimate.

4 Record the weather: sunny/cloudy; windy/still; humid/dry.

5 What colors do you see?

6 What animals pass by? Remember, humans are animals, too!

7 What flowers are open?

8 Close your eyes and listen. What do you hear?

9 Did anything unexpected happen while you were listening?

10 Draw something about the scene that fascinates you. You can draw the entire scene or one small bug, it's up to you.

11 Next time, sit in a slightly different spot to capture different observations.

The sketch of the swing and lighthouse is one of a series of lighthouse views I have painted in Marblehead, Massachusetts. One challenge of drawing the same subject over days or weeks is the temptation to stand in the same place every time. So, for this sketch, I hiked out to a local island at low tide to change things up.

Across the Harbor, ink contour drawing and watercolor, 7 x 5 inches

CITIZEN SCIENCE

You can track your observations as a citizen scientist, and you can share them with others, too. These are national free databases that welcome data from citizen scientists.

Project Budburst is one place to get going online with the phenology of the seasons.

eBird from the Cornell Lab of Ornithology lets you share bird sightings in real time and explore bird hotspots around the world.

Foldscope is a paper microscope that you build yourself. It may sound fragile, but a Foldscope is powerful enough to magnify plant cells and detect bacteria in water. Their online community collects microscopic observations from schools and individual kids.

Zooniverse.org runs on people-powered research, volunteers who help scientists study galaxies, old handwritten research notebooks, and rainforest flowers from computers at home, worldwide.

ART AND CITIZEN SCIENCE

Lara Call Gastinger, a Virginia naturalist and botanical artist, combines her interests in a weekly perpetual journal. She says, "I keep a sketchbook to learn the plants and their habitats around me, to observe seasonal changes especially in this time of climate change, and for myself to experience peaceful meditation with pen to paper in this ever increasing digital world."

Gastinger's sketchbooks are marked off in weeks: each spread of two facing pages represents one week. Each week she draws a plant or animal on the spread and, in subsequent years, she adds new nature drawings to each spread. Over the years, she's created an artistic record of the natural world a week at a time.

TOUCHING NATURE

D O YOU HAVE A LEAF?

These three chapters are meant for families with kids eight and up or for younger child / adult pairs.

Kids 12 and older can work on these activities alone or with minimal adult help.

Make the easiest leaf prints ever in the next chapter, **Chapter 9**, using only a leaf and watercolors you have at home. This is a great chapter for kids as young as eight to try independently.

Chapters 10 through **12** teach families how to print from nature using printer's ink. Believe it or not, you can print a whole fish or a leaf onto a t-shirt, and create wearable, washable art.

CHAPTER 9

WATERCOLOR LEAF PRINTS

*White oak leaves painted with watercolor and
printed by hand on copy paper.*

STARTING

Age 6 with adult help, age 8 alone

BEST IN

Spring for fresh leaves and flowers

Summer for leaves everywhere: in the garden, in a park, surrounding you on a camping trip

Fall for fallen leaves

Winter for dried leaves and seed heads of grasses

WHERE

Outdoors in the shade or indoors

TIME

Once you have a flat leaf, making a print takes five minutes

MAKE THE EASIEST LEAF PRINTS EVER! Print with watercolor paint on copy paper using leaves you collect on a quick walk outside.

You need

Watercolor paint or watercolor crayons. An inexpensive set of children's watercolors is perfect, you don't need anything fancy to make a great print!

Paintbrush

Paper (copy paper is fine)

Paper towels

Container for water, (plastic is safest)

Zipper top bag, any size

Take a walk and collect flat leaves.

I bring a zipper top bag with me on my walks, and I lay all my leaves flat inside it. When I get home, I exhale into the bag before I zip it shut, and I store it flat in the crisper drawer of the refrigerator. My breath gives the leaves carbon dioxide, and that keeps them fresh for up to a week.

Leaves from these common street trees print well: sycamore, maple, and oak. Leaves from common plants and grasses print well, too, including clover, ferns and mint.

Thick, shiny leaves, like those from a holly or magnolia, don't print as well because the watercolor can't stick to them. But torn leaves, or leaves with holes can make wonderful prints, so try everything else that catches your eye. The *PlantNet* free app identifies leaves from your photo, and *Leaf-id.com* identifies leaves by shape.

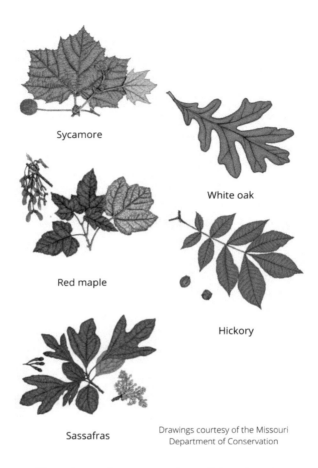

Sycamore

White oak

Red maple

Hickory

Sassafras

Drawings courtesy of the Missouri
Department of Conservation

*These leaves from trees print well, but they are
not the only ones that do!*

Learn to identify and avoid collecting the poisonous plants in your area, such as the "leaves of three, let it be" of poison ivy.

Let's print

Back inside or outside at a picnic table...choose your leaf

and look at both sides: one side will be smoother, and the other will be rougher. The rougher side, the side with the veins, is the one to paint.

- *Wet your paintbrush* with clean water

- *Rub the wet brush hard* into your favorite watercolor, really cover the wet brush with thick paint

- *Paint the entire surface* of the leaf. Even if the paint beads up on the surface of the leaf, that's ok. Add other colors as you wish, lightly touching the leaf with a paintbrush wet with a different watercolor, mixing some of this new color into the original

- *Lay a piece of copy paper* onto the wet leaf and rub. Don't forget to rub (and paint) the stem!

- *Lift off the leaf,* and you're done

Make a leaf sandwich!

- Each child needs two pieces of copy paper

- Paint both sides of a leaf, holding it by its stem

- Place the leaf onto one of the sheets of paper, cover with the second sheet, and rub...don't forget the stem!

- Life off the top sheet, the leaf, and look at the double print you have just made, front and back of your leaf.

Fern and sweetshrub leaves hand printed with watercolor.

VARIATION

Try rubbing the paintbrush into a drop of dish soap before rubbing it into the watercolor. The dish soap breaks down the waxy coating on the leaf and gives a different texture to the print.

CHAPTER 10

LEAF PRINTS WITH STICKY INK

AT THE DOORWAY OF NATURE AND ART

*Three ferns, a maple and a sassafras leaf, printed in a
walking press on Sumi-e calligraphy paper, 12 x 18 inches.*

STARTING

Age 8 with adult help, age 12 alone

BEST IN

Spring for fresh leaves and flowers

Summer for leaves everywhere: in the garden, in a park, surrounding you on a camping trip

Fall for fallen leaves

Winter for dried leaves and seed heads of grasses

WHERE

Outdoors in the shade or indoors

TIME

Once you have a flat leaf, making a print takes five minutes

A s a doorway between nature and art, leaf printing has it all: the open invitation to go outside, a chance to learn the names of trees surrounding us, and the chance to play with ink and make art. When you're printing from leaves, every leaf looks and feels differently, the hand-shaped oak leaves are stiff and opaque, and thin willow leaves are translucent and flexible.

If you tried watercolor printing in **Chapter 9,** you know how quick and satisfying leaf printing can be. This chapter takes you to the next step in printing by hand: using sticky printing ink in place of watercolor.

• *Printer's ink* allows you to create images with the precise details you can see in the *Three Ferns* print. These printer's inks are vivid and permanent when dry although, like watercolor, they wash off skin and clothes with regular soap and water.

• *Collect flat leaves anytime you go outside.* Fifteen minutes in your backyard is as good as a hike in the forest for collecting leaves. And there's no need to wait for fall to find leaves on the ground: look after a storm or on a windy day to find unusual leaves blown in on the wind. Look for flat leaves of any color and search for leaves of different shapes. Leaves with many veins, like oak, maple and dogwood, print better than very smooth ones (banana, palm, holly) because the veins in a leaf capture the printing ink.

Your prints are a visual journal of your family's walks, and searching for unusual leaves can become a family game. The *PlantNet free app* can identify leaves from your photo, and *Leaf-id.com* identifies leaves by shape.

At the end of **Chapter 9** is an image of several tree leaves that print in unusual shapes.

• You can save your leaves for up to a month by storing them in a zipper plastic bag (with a damp paper towel inside) in the crisper of your refrigerator. Tuck a bag into your suitcase when you travel and you can bring home unique leaves from your trip.

For these projects, you'll need a table. Cover the table with an old tablecloth or layer of newspaper.

You'll also need a bucket with clean water or access to a sink for washing hands when the project is complete.

While younger kids will need the help of an adult or older sibling to make these prints, older kids can make wonderful prints on their own.

Supplies

Speedball printing ink and extender are non-toxic and wash up easily with water. One 2.5 oz. tube is enough for 25-30 prints and costs less than $5 at local art supply stores or online at Dick Blick or Amazon. You will find pads of Sumi-e (**soo**-me-ee) calligraphy paper there too. Thai unryu (un-**rye**-you) paper, another printmaker's paper that is strong and translucent, comes in many colors besides white. You can find it online at Blick or GPC Papers, and in many brick and mortar art stores.

Basic printmaking supplies: water-based printer's ink, paper, paintbrush, brayer, paper plate for rolling out ink.

You need

Flat leaves

Two or three 2.5 oz. tubes Speedball water-soluble printing ink in colors such as silver, red and green

Copy paper, several sheets per person

OR 1 pad of 12 x 18 Sumi-e calligraphy paper (or

other paper meant for calligraphy or printing such as Thai unryu.)

One flat 1 inch or 1/2 inch wide watercolor paintbrush, or one foam brush

White paper plates as a place to roll out the ink. Colored plates won't let you see the actual color of your ink.

OR Freezer paper (from the grocery store) If using freezer paper, tape a 12+ inch piece of it onto the table covering, and tape down the table covering so you can roll out the ink.

Paper towels

A place to hang or lay the leaf prints to dry for an hour

Optional supplies

One 1.25 oz. tube Speedball ink retarder to slow down the drying time of the ink. If you are printing outside or in a winter-dry room, the ink can dry before you have a chance to print. One tube is enough for a day of printing. Squeeze out retarder in a blob the size of half a dime and mix it into the ink before you roll it out.

One 4 inch foam paint roller or soft brayer to apply ink. You can find the paint roller at a hardware store in the paint department marked as a "trim" roller. You'll find the brayer at Dick Blick or any art supply store.

Let's start

1 Choose your leaf. Place it rough side up on the newspaper surface. The rough side is the side with the most prominent veins.

2 Mix the ink. Squeeze out a quarter-sized blob of each color of ink on a separate plate or place on the freezer paper. Printing ink is really, really sticky and you need very little to make a great print. If you are using retarder, mix a half dime-sized blob into the ink.

Have fun mixing colors with your brush or brayer on the leaf. You can also mix colors with your brush or brayer on the paper plate or freezer paper palette and then apply them to the leaf. For realistic color, add silver to your ink mix; for more primary, vivid color, leave it out.

You are the artist! You can use any colors you like in your prints.

If you are using a paintbrush to apply ink, read A.

If you are using a brayer to apply ink, read B.

A Using a paintbrush, spread ink on the rough side of the leaf in a thin, translucent layer. Go slowly, dabbing different colors of ink on the veins and stem, perhaps. Enjoy the silky feeling of the ink and the texture of the leaf as you lightly cover the surface with ink.

B Use the 4 inch brayer or 4 inch sponge paint roller to apply ink to the leaf. You will create sharper prints that show more detail, because the brayer applies ink in thinner layers than the paintbrush.

To do this, roll the brayer into the ink, picking up ink and rolling away from you to cover the brayer completely.

Gently roll the inked brayer over the leaf. Remember to cover the edges of the leaf, its stem, and the areas between its veins, as much as possible.

4 Move the leaf to a clean place on the newsprint, ink side up.

5 Wipe your hands. You don't want a print of your fingers!

6 Lay copy or rice paper on top of the leaf and rub gently using the palm of your hand and your fingertips. Use copy paper to make the first print from a new leaf. Once you have the hang of printing, try rice paper for later prints. You might also use the first print to test color combinations that you can then refine for later prints.

7 Lift off the printing paper, leaving the leaf on the newspaper below. You have a leaf print!

If you ink new leaves, you can make multiple prints on the same sheet of paper. Your prints will be dry to the touch in two hours. At that point, you can add the *Variations,* below, or simply tack it to the wall and enjoy.

TROUBLESHOOTING

Is your first print faint?

You might have inked too lightly. A faint, spotty print showing few details has too little ink--next time you can spread the ink with a heavier hand.

What if the print looks thick and blotchy?

Less ink is more! Next time, use half the amount of ink you think you need: think of a feather of ink laying on the surface of the leaf. You can use many different colors of ink as long as you apply them lightly.

Oak-leaf hydrangea, sassafras and gum leaves,
monoprint on paper, 14 x 11 inches

VARIATIONS

Make a sandwich print. This method gives you a two-sided print: you are printing the front and back of a leaf at the same time. You'll need a second sheet of paper and, possibly, a pair of tweezers.

1 Choose your leaf and lay out two clean sheets of paper.

2 Mix the ink. Squeeze out a 1 inch ribbon of each color of ink on a plate or freezer paper. Mix in the optional retarder if you are printing outside.

3 Using a brush or brayer, paint a rectangle of ink onto the freezer paper, a rectangle that is larger than your leaf. You can use one or combine many colors.

4 Lay the leaf flat onto this rectangle. The bottom side of the leaf is receiving ink as you press down.

5 Using a brush or a brayer, spread ink on the top side of the leaf. Now the leaf is inked on both sides.

6 Pick up the leaf by the stem with your fingertips or with a tweezer and lay it flat on a clean sheet of paper.

7 Wipe your hands.

8 Cover the leaf with the second sheet of paper and rub gently, feeling for the stem, the margins of the leaf, and the center of the leaf where the stem joins the body.

9 Lift off the cover sheet and peel the inky leaf off the paper using tweezers or your fingers.

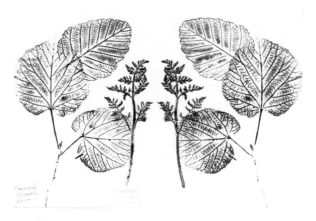

Basswood and cow parsley, monoprint, 8 x 11 inches

Add color

Bird of paradise leaf printed, then colored by hand
with inky brayers and Caran d'ache pastel,
monoprint on paper, 10 x 14 inches.

When the print is dry, use dry media—crayons, pastels colored pencils—to add extra color. Wet media, such as magic markers or paint, will make thin printing paper wrinkle and will soak through the print.

When you print with ink, don't let the realistic color of a leaf hold you back—use fanciful color too. Inking your leaves in multiple colors makes for energetic prints.

Add flowers or fruit

To print with flowers you can use the same method. Flatter ones, like dandelions, print well, while full blossoms, like roses, are difficult to capture in a print. But, you can print some of the individual petals from a large or full flower, especially if they are crinkled and full of texture themselves.

To print with flowers, flatten them overnight.

• Clip each stem very short and place the flowers or petals *face up or down* on newspaper under several heavy books. In the morning, they will be flat enough to print with.

To print with fruit or vegetables, cut them in thin slices.

• *For example, if you are cutting a lemon, cut it in half* on the short side, including the rind. Then, cut a slice about 1/2 inch thick from this cut and lay the slice on its side on paper towels or newspaper to dry overnight. In the morning, this slice will be dry enough to print with. Donna Fay Allen of the Nature Printing Society created wrapping paper using fruits and vegetables and several colors of printing ink.

Orange slice and spiral stamp printed on white paper. Photo courtesy D.F. Allen.

Experiment with papers

Old grocery bags, Japanese rice papers, Thai collage papers...you can even stamp on a flat fabric lampshade. A good printing surface is one that absorbs ink (otherwise it will stay wet forever!).

Avoid printing on plastic surfaces or cloth with this water-based ink. To print on t-shirts or any fabric see **Chapter 12 Wear Your Prints!**

Old newspaper should be a great surface for prints: it is absorbent and the letters themselves make a fascinating background. But newspaper turns yellow fast because it isn't acid-free. Use it to make your test prints, but don't rely on it for your final ones.

Use a walking press

Chapter 13 explains how to build and use a walking press, a home-built printing press that uses body weight to make prints on paper and cloth. Prints made in a walking press have wonderful detail.

Because a walking press is large, often three feet wide and long, you can lay out and print a large arrangement of leaves at one time.

The image of ferns at the start of this chapter was printed using a walking press.

GOOD TO KNOW

If I had a...what?

• *Try a hammer* to make your next leaf prints. The Japanese call this technique *tataki zome* or flower pounding. It's based on the idea that most leaves and flowers contain enough pigment to make prints when you pound them onto cloth or paper using a rubber mallet or regular metal hammer. The colors in these natural prints will be bright and the pounded prints will show amazing detail.

Three pansy prints made by tataki zome and one real pansy before pounding.

•. You can use flower pounding to hide stains on beloved shirts. You can use it to create a huge design with a group (such as a forest floor or group mandala) on a muslin banner or tarp from the hardware store. It's satisfying, energetic, and loud method of printmaking, great to use on a rainy afternoon in the garage or on a covered patio.

• But, like a favorite fall leaf, tataki zome prints eventually fade. These natural pigments can't withstand much daily light or washing. You can accept this and simply print over faded prints again and again.

Or, you can take a photo of a particularly good pounded print to keep it alive with its most vivid colors. Using the image, you can go on to create cards or even a tablecloth by scanning your print and sending it out to be printed on cloth using a service such as Spoonflower.

• All you need to make these prints is a hammer or rubber mallet, a leaf or flower, a paper towel, and a piece of copy paper or white handkerchief.

1 Place your paper or cloth on a flat rock or sidewalk.

2 Place leaves on top of the paper or cloth. Don't overlap the leaves, because they won't print clearly. Ferns print particularly well when you print them with a hammer. Flat flowers, such as pansies, can be pounded all at once.

If you have a flower with many overlapping petals, such as a daisy, remove all the petals, place each petal on the paper in the characteristic shape of the flower and pound that image instead.

3 Place the paper towel on top of the leaves or flowers.

4 Pound the leaves through the paper towel until you think you have pounded all the leaves. You will see the faint outline of the leaf or flower emerge on the paper towel as you pound.

5 Lift the paper towel and the leaves. You have leaf prints in beautiful colors.

CHAPTER 11

FISH PRINTS

SLIPPERY, SCALY FISH MAKE PERFECT SUBJECTS FOR
NATURE PRINTS

STARTING

Age 8 with adult help, age 12 alone

BEST IN

Spring and early summer for migrating fish, such as salmon or shad

Summer for the fish you catch yourself

Fall and winter for whole fish you find at the grocery store

WHERE

Outdoors in the shade or indoors

TIME

Once you have a clean fish, a print takes 10 minutes; washing and drying the fish takes 10 minutes

THOSE WHOLE FISH at the grocery store—who knew you could use them for more than dinner?

Whether your family fishes together, or whether you buy your fish at the grocery store, everyone can print a fish in the style of the Japanese *gyotaku* masters, artists who create fish prints by printing on paper or silk. Fish of any size, from the five-inch butterfish in the print above, to ten-inch trout, to eight-foot octopus make great prints because scales, fins and suckers catch the ink and release it to the paper.

If you've already printed leaves, you'll find the basic steps of fish printing familiar. Different, of course, is the preparation of the fish itself. While the details are below, you'll be washing the whole fish in a sink or outside under a hose, propping up the fins and tail of the fish to make a level printing surface, and leaving it to air dry on a table for ten minutes before you print. You **do not** scale or gut the fish before printing.

You're in touch with nature in an immediate and sometimes smelly way in fish printing. As you wipe ink on the fish, the roughness and shape of its body will tell you if it is a fast or slow swimmer: a fast swimmer has a smooth torpedo-shaped body and pointed fins (think mackerel), and a slow swimmer has a less-smooth round body and rounded fins (think carp).

This fish is a shiner, a common bait fish.

A fish uses its lateral line to sense vibration in the surrounding water. Although the lateral line is almost invis-ible in a fresh fish, it often prints distinctly.

Fresh fish have bright red gills and transparent eyes. The eye will look clear and rounded as in the image of the shiner, not sunken or red. While it's easy to imagine the large scales of a carp making a dramatic print, even the tiny scales of a flounder catch ink and will make a beautiful image. And, as you catch the gyotaku (gee-o-**tah**-ku) bug, you'll find yourself experimenting on oysters, on squid, even on lobster and crab shells.

Supplies

Choosing fish. Start with a fish weighing less than two pounds. A fish of this size will fit on the recommended paper and will be easy to clean at the kitchen sink or outside under the hose. As everyone becomes comfortable with the fish print process, you will want to experiment with fish of all sizes. Kids love printing the flat flounder with the two eyes positioned on top.

The fish should be very fresh, whole, un-gutted, unscaled, with its tail and all of its fins. I find regional and imported whole fish at my local Asian grocery store and the prints in this chapter were made from fish I found there. One fish will make at least 10 prints if handled gently.

Select a fish with a flat body for your first prints; see *Fish that print well,* at the end of the chapter, on how to choose a good-printing fish.

Choosing ink and paper. Water-based, non-toxic Speedball ink is available online at Dick Blick or Amazon or in local art supply stores for less than $5 per tube. You'll find pads of Sumi-e calligraphy paper there, too. A more expensive paper made with swirls of white fibers is Thai unryu, another printmaker's paper that is strong and translucent. You can find it online at Blick or GPC Papers, and in many brick and mortar art stores.

Set up the art space. For this project, you'll need a place to wash hands and a table. Cover the table with two layers of newspaper. Bring the printing paper and the paper towels within arm's reach. For your mixing palette, set out a paper plate (or tape down a 16" length of freezer paper to your table).

You need

A fish weighing less than 2 pounds

Dishwashing soap or **regular table salt,** no fancy salt needed

Two 2.5 oz. tubes Speedball water-soluble printing ink (2 different colors such as silver and blue)

Speedball ink extender, 1 tube

2 paintbrushes, one with a tiny point (such as size 1 or 0) for painting in the eye of the fish

1 pad newsprint for the first prints (8 x 10 pad or larger)

OR newspaper

1 pad of 12 x 18 calligraphy paper , such as Sumi-e (for later prints with more detail)

White paper plates (colored paper plates won't let you see the actual color of your ink)

OR freezer paper (from any grocery store) and **tape**

Paper towels

Table covering (more newspaper, or an old tablecloth)

A place to hang or lay the fish prints to dry for an hour

Camera

Let's start

1 If you're a fisherman (or know one) use your catch. Otherwise, you'll find the largest assortment of whole fish at a grocery store. Your fish can be fresh or thawed. Asian markets often have a large selection of whole fresh and frozen fish, including squid and octopi. If you're heading to the grocery store, you can buy the fish a day ahead and store it in the coldest part of your refrigerator overnight.

This fish isn't edible after printing. Most likely, it will have been touched by many hands and it will have sat out, unrefrigerated, for several hours.

2 Wash your fish gently at home in the kitchen sink or outside under a gentle trickle from the hose. Use a quart of cool water mixed with a tablespoon of dish-washing liquid for the first rinse. Then, sprinkle a tablespoon of salt over one side of the fish and gently wipe it away with a damp paper towel. Repeat on the other side of the fish. This removes the protective mucus of the fish. Finally, rinse the entire fish in cool water. Some fish, such as carp, have lots of mucus, so you might need to wash them twice.

· · ·

3 Take a photo of the fish, if you can. The photo will help you remember the original colors of the fish and the detail of its eye. You can refer back to this picture later when you are drawing or painting in the fish eye.

4 Let your fish dry, uncovered, for at least 10 minutes and up to a few hours. Open all the fins and dry them with a paper towel. Work slowly as you do: sometimes fins contain hidden spines, which the living fish uses for defense in the ocean.

- A dry fish makes a better print. The gills can leak water onto the print so, if they are not too small and inaccessible, plug them with a sliver of folded paper towel.

- Use a sliver of paper towel to *plug the anal vent,* too, if it is leaking.

- If the gills or anal vent do leak and stain the print, it is easy to fix. First, wait until the print dries. Often the stain fades away when the liquid evaporates.

- If the stain is still there once the print has dried, **and with the help of an adult**, mix a solution of 50/50 bleach and water in a disposable cup. Using a cotton swab, dab the liquid on the stain and let dry. The stain should fade or disappear after this treatment.

5 Mix the ink. Squeeze out a blob of each color the size of a quarter on a plate or the freezer paper. Printing ink is really, really sticky and you need very little to make a great print.

Touch the ink on your mixing palette with a finger. If you hear a faint "snap" when you pull your finger away, the ink is ready to use. If you have trouble pulling your finger away, the ink is too stiff. Add a dab more extender to the color and mix with your finger or with a paintbrush.

6 Using the paintbrush, spread ink on the fish in a thin layer beginning with the head. Go slowly and feel the edges of scales and the hard smoothness of the head.

> • *Don't ink the fish's eye.* You will paint or draw it in later on the print itself.

> • Carefully ink the fins, watching for spines. Enjoy the silky feeling of the ink as you brush it onto the fish.

> • *Wipe your hands* when you finish inking the fish.

7 Move your fish to a clean place on the newspaper. Prop up fins using paper towels underneath the body of the fish. If your fish has a round body, like the carp, below, prop up its tail with torn newspaper or crumpled paper towels to bring it to the height of the round body. It will print without distortion if you do this. You can also position the fish's body in a curve or experiment with opening its mouth to create an expression.

Wipe your hands again.

Printing the tail of a carp, propped up with paper towels. This carp has a shiny oval eye. I used this fish for demonstration, so it is large, almost eight pounds.

8 Print the fish. Using both hands, lay newsprint or rice paper on top of the fish. The printing ink is sticky, so, once the paper is down, don't move it, or you will leave an ink smudge on the paper.

- *Beginning at the head,* gently press the paper onto the inked fish. Avoid pressing the eye. As you reach the mouth, go slowly, trying to capture the last detail of the fish's expression in the shape of its mouth.

- *Move on to printing the "landmark" fins,* the dorsal, pectoral and ventral fins. The dorsal is at the top of the fish, the pectoral near the gill, and the ventral along the bottom.

- *Create a "fin sandwich"* by placing one hand underneath the fin and the other hand on top of the paper covering the fin. Press and rub the fin between your two hands, taking care to avoid any dorsal or ventral spines.

- *Next, print the fish's body* by moving your hands diagonally across it, pressing lightly. The diagonal movement helps you to keep the appearance of roundness in the print of the fish's body.

• *As you reach the edges* of the fish's body, create a sharp edge by pressing down onto the paper with your fingernail. This crispness is one marker of a professional fish print.

Printing the tail of the carp. You can see its large scales through the translucent Sumi-e paper.

9 Lift off the paper, beginning at the head. You have a fish print!

Your print will be dry to the touch in an hour. Then you'll be ready to *Add the eye* and other *Variations*, below.

Troubleshooting

You might have inked too lightly: A faint, spotty print showing few details has too little ink--next time, gather more ink on your brush and remember to refill it.

If, on the other hand, *you inked too heavily*, your print looks blotchy and you can't see any details. Next time, use half the amount of ink you think you need: imagine a thin skin of ink resting on the surface of the fish. You can combine many different colors of ink on the brush or on the body of the fish as long as you apply them lightly.

VARIATIONS

Add an eye

Rockfish on silk, monoprint (indirect gyotaku),
18 x 16 inches

It's easy to draw or paint in the eye of your fish. That eye, with a tiny reflection added, brings the whole print to life. It's likely that you already have a white space on your print showing you where the eye painting or drawing will go, and you can see that white eye space in the top fish in the rockfish print. If you took a photo of your fish before you began printing, you can refer to it to see the original shape of the eye.

To practice drawing eyes, all you need is a pencil.

• This is often where people freeze, saying to themselves, "I can't paint a fish eye!" Don't panic.

• Practice these steps on scrap paper first to loosen up.

• Tell yourself you are simply drawing shapes. Look at the fish eye itself or at the photo you took before you began printing. Use a light pencil line to draw the outline of the iris and the pupil of the eye on the print. Draw in the outline of the white reflection in the pupil, too.

• Lightly shade in the darker parts of the iris. Make the pupil, except for the reflection, the darkest part of the eye. Leave the reflection unshaded.

• You can also use the tiny brush and printing ink to paint the eye onto the print. Again, the pupil will be the darkest, and the reflection will stay unpainted. Use a light touch and practice first on scrap paper.

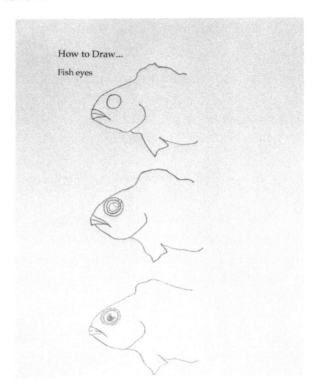

How to Draw...

Fish eyes

Add a ghost print

Many fish retain extra ink after an initial print. You can print them again without adding additional ink and create a "ghost" print. This second print will be lighter in color than the first.

If you make a ghost print on the same sheet of paper you printed your first fish on, your print will look three dimensional: the dark fish, printed first, will come forward and the light ghost, printed second, will appear to swim in the background. I printed the image of the school of fish that opens this chapter using ghost printing.

.   .   .

Add atmosphere

You can print seaweed or sponges on the fish print to give it a lively background. You might print these first and overlap them with a fish print to give a three dimensional effect.

If it is hard to find seaweed where you live, many evergreens from your backyard have needles or leaflets that, when printed, resemble seaweed. I print with small branches from the Hinoki and Leyland cypress when I can't find seaweed. See the image of a flounder printed with Leyland cypress in **Chapter 13.**

Print on different papers

Printmakers need absorbent paper. Any thin paper marked "printmaking" at an art supply store will give great results for fish prints.

Sumi-e and Thai unryu are two widely known types of paper but you can experiment with printing on paper bags, Kraft paper, and colored mulberry or so-called rice paper. In **Chapter 12,** you can even experiment with printing on cloth.

The original gyotaku artists printed their catch on newspaper because it was cheap and handy. Newspaper and newsprint aren't acid free, meaning over time the paper will turn yellow and brittle. But, they absorb ink beautifully and are wonderful papers to use for initial prints with a new fish. If you happen to make a beautiful print with these papers, you can take a photograph of the print before it yellows and use the photo for a card or in a calendar.

Matting and display

If you mat your work, suddenly you'll have real art. You can mount your print to a slightly larger sheet of colored construction paper for an informal look.

For a more formal look, select a mat with an opening the size of your print. Most mats include a backing board. Place the print facing out of the mat window and tape the print in place. Tape the backing board in place, sandwiching the print inside. Finally, use an easel back (a cardboard stand available at art supply or craft stores) to stand it up for display.

GOOD TO KNOW: Hints for adults and older kids

Storing and freezing fish

If you are printing within 48 hours of purchasing the fish, store it in the refrigerator, inside a plastic bag. Put newspaper or paper towels under the bag to absorb any leaking fluid from the fish.

• Otherwise, *clean and freeze the fish* until you are ready to print. Clean the fish as above, using dish soap, salt and water. To freeze, wrap the fish in a layer of plastic wrap, seal inside a zipper freezer bag, and label it with the date and type of fish. If your fish is too large for a bag, wrap it in plastic wrap and them wrap it in freezer paper, taping it closed around the wrapped fish.

. . .

• When you are ready to print, *thaw the fish,* allowing at least a day for a two-pound fish to thaw in the refrigerator. Place the bag holding the thawing fish on paper towels in the refrigerator, even if you think your bag is sealed. When your fish is thawed, place it on newsprint, pat it dry and leave it unrefrigerated and uncovered for at least 10 minutes. A dry fish will make a better print.

• You might have an unusual fish, one that has printed particularly well or that is unique in size or type. *You can refreeze it and reuse it for several cycles.*

One member of the Nature Printing Society has frozen and re-frozen an eight-foot octopus given to her by Alaskan fishermen who found it tangled in a tuna net, and she has been able to print from it for several years by carefully wrapping and freezing it.

• The Nature Printing Society is the primary resource for information on fish printing worldwide. Adults can sign up for the autumn conference where you can learn expert techniques in fish and nature printing. Can't make it to the conference? You can join NPS and receive the quarterly newsletter or purchase its book *The Art of Printing From Nature.*

Fish that print well...and don't

• *Choose local fish whenever you can.* I print protected fish, like the mid-Atlantic's rockfish, from time to time, but I practice my technique on plentiful, inexpensive fish. To print unusual varieties or sizes of fish, you can contact a local fish distributor who can help you find unique fish sizes and varieties.

• *The easiest fish to print have flat bodies.* Here on the Chesapeake Bay, near where I live, those fish include spot, white bass and flounder. Butterfish are plentiful along the east coast of the U.S. and they also come frozen in other parts of the U.S. All these fish are easy to find at a local market and can be reused to make many prints--they are tough!

• *Many rounder-bodied fish, like trout, bass, shad and grouper make great prints* because they have prominent scales. You will need to prop up their tails and fins to create a flat body surface for printing. This is easy to do if you prop up their fins using crumpled newsprint, paper towels, or balls of soft clay.

• *Squid and octopus are wonderful!* Don't let their fragile appearance fool you—they print beautifully and make expressive prints with their long tentacles. If you purchase them frozen, let them thaw overnight in the refrigerator before you print with them. You only need to rinse them in cool water once they are thawed, they are not slimy and do not need to be rubbed with salt or dish soap.

• *Avoid mackerel and other torpedo-shaped fish if you're new to fish printing.* Their bodies are built for speed, they're muscular and almost scale-free. They won't print well.

GOOD TO KNOW

If you are (or know) a fisherman and you print your catch, you're continuing a long tradition: Japanese fishermen in the pre-photography days of the mid-1800s recorded the size of their catch by using soot-based sumi ink to print the size of the fish on mulberry paper. After quick printing, they rinsed off this water-based ink in the sea and ate their catch. The Japanese named these prints *gyotaku*: *gyo* for fish and *taku* for print. Gyotaku is now considered an art form both in Japan and around the world.

*Celestial Koi, hand-printed gyotaku by Dwight
Hwang, sumi ink on paper*

Here in the U.S., Dwight Hwang continues this distin-
guished tradition. He prints with sumi ink, which is thinner
and less sticky than printmaking ink, and he must print
quickly before the ink dries. Dwight's energetic and beautiful compositions have been adapted for book covers and
posters.

CHAPTER 12

WEAR YOUR PRINTS!

LEAF AND FISH PRINTS ON CLOTH MAKE WEARABLE, WASHABLE ART

T-shirt hand printed using a walking press.

STARTING

This is a family project. With adults or older kids helping, children as young as 6 can have fun printing t-shirts. Kids 12 and up can do this on their own may only need a bit of adult help to gather the supplies.

BEST IN

Any season for fish you catch or find at the grocery store

Spring through fall for leaves

WHERE

Outside in the shade or indoors

TIME

An afternoon: 2-4 hours

T-SHIRTS, APRONS, HATS, SCARVES…you can print on anything made of at least 50% cotton or silk.

Do you have a spot on your favorite shirt? Cover it up with a nature print and you can wear it a bit longer! You will find supplies for this project at your local hardware and grocery stores and art supplies online at Amazon and Dick Blick.

You can finish this project in one day or work on it over several, and they don't have to be back-to-back. For convenience, the directions are broken down into a three-day timeline, but you can print leaf t-shirts in an afternoon.

If you are new to T-shirt printing, I suggest you begin with leaf printing.

On day one, take a walk and collect your leaves or purchase your fish. Cut cardboard or freezer paper to size to make an insert for the t-shirt to prevent the printing ink from bleeding through to the back side.

On day two, print the t-shirt. The printing process itself takes about 20 minutes. Put the shirt aside until the ink is dry, which takes eight hours or overnight.

On day three, heat set the print.

Summer shirt hand printed with leaves

SUPPLIES NEEDED FOR BOTH LEAF AND FISH PRINTING ON FABRIC

White or light-colored cotton t-shirt (or scarf, or apron)

- Are you printing a new shirt? If so, wash, dry (and possibly iron) your fabric to remove the factory-applied sizing and flatten the cloth before you print.

Cardboard insert the width of your shirt, how-to, below

OR Freezer paper cut to the width of your shirt **and masking tape** to tape it down to the table

4 oz. jars of Luminere Versetex fabric printing ink

2 oz. bottle Versetex ink fixer

One plastic spoon per color

- This fabric ink and the ink fixer are non-toxic and clean up with soap and water.

- You may find tempting assortment packages of eight small jars online, but don't buy them. These packages contain too many similar colors.

- *Try the 4 oz. size* of Golden Yellow, Sky Blue, Magenta, Turquoise and Super Opaque White to make colorful prints on white or dark fabric. The turquoise and the golden yellow make a gorgeous green when mixed together, and the turquoise and magenta make a dark, almost black ink.

• *Where's the red?* You can mix a beautiful red by mixing a bit of magenta with a lot of golden yellow.

Newsprint or newspaper

Paper plate, one for each color

OR Freezer paper, 12 to 48 inches cut and taped to your table, to use as a surface for rolling out ink

Paper towels

Tweezers

A place to hang or lay the t-shirt to dry

Iron and towels for heat setting the shirt

Camera

SPECIAL SUPPLIES FOR LEAF PRINTING

Flat leaves

• Flat leaves are easiest to print and any flat leaf is worth a try. You'll find that thick leaves with distinctive veins make the best prints: try sycamore, maple, oak, dogwood or gingko to start. Leaves with shiny, waxy surfaces, like magnolia or holly or eucalyptus are harder to print.

• Store your leaves flat in the refrigerator in a zipper lock bag until you are ready to print. Exhale into the bag before you zip it shut, the carbon dioxide of your breath will help the leaves stay fresh until you need them.

• For pictures of leaves that print well and for information on choosing them, see **Chapters 9** and **10.**

Four-inch foam rollers from the paint section of a hardware store.

• Buy one roller for each color and one or two extra for the colors you mix yourself, such as green.

• Wash the rollers with dish soap and water and leave them to air dry when you are finished printing. Foam rollers can be reused many times before they start to wear out.

• If you will be printing another shirt within the next month, you can avoid washing the rollers for now by storing them in a zipper lock bag. When you are ready to print again, they will be moist and ready to reuse.

SPECIAL SUPPLIES FOR FISH PRINTING

1.5 inch bristle paint brushes from the hardware store, one for each color

A tiny pointed paintbrush (size 0 or one)

LEAF PRINTING

DAY 1

1 Measure and cut a cardboard insert from an old

box to fit inside the shirt, filling it from side-to-side. This insert prevents the print's wet ink from bleeding through to other side of the shirt. It also keeps the front of the shirt from twisting so you can make a straight, centered print. Save the insert to use again whenever you print t-shirts.

If you are printing on a canvas bag, the cardboard will help the cloth stay flat as you print. Place the insert inside the bag.

2 Take a walk and choose your leaves. Store them flat in a zipper top bag in the refrigerator.

DAY 2

1 Set up the printing space. Lay out:

- One paper plate for each color of ink **OR** tape down a big palette of freezer paper, shiny side up.

- One roller for each color of ink

- A tube of ink next to each roller

- One spoon per color of ink

- Paper towels

- Leaves

- The shirt you will be printing on

2 Spoon out a blob of ink the size of a quarter for each color onto the paper plate or freezer paper. Add ink fixer to each color, if you are using it, according to the instructions on the bottle. *If you use fixer, you do not need to heat set the printed fabric when you are finished.*

3 Using one foam roller for each color, roll out the ink on each paper plate or on the freezer paper, covering the roller completely.

4 For your first prints, choose leaves with simple solid shapes, such as oak, maple, or sycamore. Look at the two sides of your leaf: each will print differently. Usually, the top side of a leaf is smoother than the underside. The underside, the side with the veins, will print with the most detail.

5 Roll the lightest color of ink onto the leaf first. You can print this leaf now or add other colors on top of the first color. Printmakers struggle to keep their brayers clean, their colors separate, and the only way to manage is to roll light colors, such as yellow, on the leaf first and then add darker colors on top.

• If you roll blue on first, then yellow, the yellow brayer would pick up the blue ink and turn green right away.

• The blue ink has more covering power and will stay blue for quite a while.

• So, to produce green, roll yellow, then blue onto the leaf

• For orange, roll yellow, then red or magenta onto the leaf

• For purple, roll magenta, than roll a bit of blue

Experiment with rolling light colors on top of dark ones, for example, yellow on top of blue, with one of the extra rollers.

- Go slowly, perhaps rolling a new color in a single swipe on the stem and veins

- When you are done applying color, wipe your hands

6 Insert the cardboard into the t-shirt.

7 Pick up an inked leaf with your fingers or tweezer and place it, ink side down, on the shirt. Lay a clean sheet of newsprint or paper towel on the leaf and rub hard, feeling for the stem, the veins and the edges of the leaf.

8 Remove the paper and lift the leaf, using tweezers. You have your first leaf print on fabric. Add more prints to finish the design you like.

FISH PRINTING

DAY 1

1 Go to the fish market and purchase a fish that weighs under two pounds, one with scales you can see. Clean the fish, rubbing it gently with salt or baking soda under cold running water, either in a sink or under a hose, using dish soap to remove slime. Carefully open and wash fins, watching for spines!

- *If you are printing today,* leave the fish out on your newspaper-covered table for at least 10 minutes, uncovered, so it can air dry and make a more distinct print. Stuff leaky gills and, possibly, anus with small pieces of rolled up paper towel to prevent them staining the cloth.

• *If you are printing tomorrow,* store the fish in a plastic bag in the refrigerator overnight. The next morning, take the fish out of the refrigerator and follow the instructions, above, for *printing today.*

2 Measure and cut a cardboard insert from an old box to fit inside the shirt, filling it from side-to-side. This insert prevents the print's wet ink from bleeding through to other side of the shirt. It also keeps the front of the shirt from twisting so you can make a straight, centered print. Save the insert to use again whenever you print t-shirts.

If you are printing on a canvas bag, the cardboard will help the cloth stay flat as you print. Place the insert inside the bag.

DAY 2

1 Set up the printing space. Lay out:

• One paper plate for each color of ink **OR** tape down a big palette of freezer paper, shiny side up.

• One roller for each color of ink

• A tube of ink next to each roller

• One spoon per color of ink

- Paper towels

- The fish, on newspaper, uncovered

- The shirt you will be printing on

2 Spoon out a blob of ink the size of a quarter for each color onto the paper plate or freezer paper. Add ink fixer to each color, if you are using it, according to the instructions on the bottle. *If you use fixer, you do not need to heat set the printed fabric when you are finished.*

3 Use one paintbrush for each color, and mix the fixer into the ink using the brush.

4 Photograph your fish before you start. Fish eyes come in many odd shapes, and few of them are perfectly round, though we tend to draw them that way in anime or quick sketches. Don't ink the fish's eye, though. You will paint it in after you have made your print.

5 Paint the fish with the ink in a thin layer starting at the head and moving toward the tail. When you finish inking on this direction, *reverse course* and lightly pass the brush over the fish from tail to head. This fills in all remaining spots on the fish with ink and gives good definition to its scales. Carefully ink the fins, watching for spines that fish use to protect themselves. Enjoy the silky flow of the ink as you cover the fish!

- *You can use more than one color of ink* to paint your fish. If you paint the fish in darker colors, such as blue, at the top of the body, and fade the colors to gray or white at the belly, you are *countershading.* Fish use countershading as camouflage to blend into the flickering light and shadow of a river or lake.

• Tropical fish live in a brilliantly sunny world, one created by sparkling patterns of light on coral and white sand. Experiment with bright colors and unusual patterns whether or not you have a tropical fish.

• *Wipe your hands* when you finish inking the fish.

6 Move your fish to a clean place on the newspaper.

• Prop open fins using paper towels underneath the body of the fish. If your fish has a round body, like the carp, below, prop up its tail with torn newspaper or crumpled paper towels to bring it to the height of the round body. It will print without distortion if you do this.

• You can also position the fish's body in a curve or experiment with opening its mouth to create an expression.

• *Wipe your hands when you have finished.*

7 Insert the cardboard into the t-shirt.

8 Insert your hands into the shirt palms against the inside of the shirt, back of your hands against the cardboard. Stretch the cloth lightly with your palms to help it lay flat.

9 Position the middle of the shirt over the fish and slowly lower the stretched cloth onto the inked fish. Press your palms, through the fabric, gently onto the fish: it will feel cool.

- Slowly move your hands toward the head of the fish, pressing gently.

- Slowly slide your hands to each landmark fin, pressing lightly to capture as much detail as possible.

- Finally, slide your hands across the entire body to the tail and press lightly to print it.

10 Slowly remove your hands from inside the shirt. Lift the shirt off the fish. Remove the cardboard. You have your first fish print on fabric! You can stop here, or ink the fish and print again, as you wish.

11 Hang the shirt to dry for at least 8 hours or overnight. Wipe off the fish to make another print, or rinse fish under clean water to repackage and freeze it for another day.

FINISHING FOR LEAVES AND FISH

DAY 3

Heat set the ink

Eight hours later (or sooner if the ink is dry) use an iron to heat-set your print so it will become permanent.

- Place a clean old towel on your ironing board and lay the printed cloth, print side down, onto the towel.

• Heat the iron to medium (no steam).

• Lay a thin dish towel over the print and press the entire back side of the print for two minutes.

Wash the printed fabric

Heat setting your fabric print means the fabric can be washed by hand. Wash the fabric using dish soap in the sink and hang the fabric to dry on a rack. I take the extra precaution of washing my hand-printed shirts inside out to preserve the print for as long as I can.

Not washing? Don't heat set

Prints don't have to be heat set if you won't be washing them. This canvas carpenter's apron turned into an art piece. I use it for display only, so I have not heat set it.

Fish overprinted by leaves on canvas carpenter's apron.

VARIATIONS

Add an eye to a fish print

It's easy to draw or paint in the eye of your fish. That eye, with a tiny reflection added, brings the whole print to life. It's likely that you already have a white space on the cloth showing you where the eye should go.

• This is often the spot where people freeze, saying to themselves, "I can't paint a fish eye!" Don't panic.

• Practice these steps on scrap paper first to loosen up.

• Tell yourself you are simply drawing shapes. Use a tiny brush and the ink you used to print the fish to draw the outline of the iris and the pupil of the eye on the cloth. Draw in the outline of the white reflection in the pupil, too.

• Lightly shade in the darker parts of the iris. Make the pupil, except for the reflection, the darkest part of the eye. Leave the reflection unshaded.

For a diagram on painting basic fish eyes, see **Chapter 11**, "How to Draw Fish Eyes".

Add words to the shirt

You can add words to your shirt by stamping them in, by using stencils, or by hand lettering using fabric paint. All methods work equally well. Keep the cardboard backing inside the shirt to stabilize it and to keep the lettering ink from staining the other side of the shirt.

You can also create a basic stencil by printing out your word or phrase onto a 8 1/2 x 11 inch mylar sheet. From there, lay the sheet on a scrap piece of cardboard or cutting mat and cut out the letters in the stencil using an exacto knife. Lay the stencil on the fabric and lightly apply ink over the letters using a brush.

This black shirt was printed with old wooden
type dipped in silver ink, then pressed onto the
shirt one letter at a time.

Print on dark fabric

You can print on colored fabric too. Metallic inks look great
on dark cloth, as does opaque white. When you print on a
colored surface, mix your ink colors with opaque white ink
to make them visible against the dark background.

Apron hand-printed with maple, ash and oak leaves.

Use a walking press

Chapter 13 explains how to build and use a walking press, a simple printing press that uses body weight to make prints on cloth or paper. A walking press is especially good at making prints on fabric and, because of the pressure of the process, prints made by this method have wonderful detail.

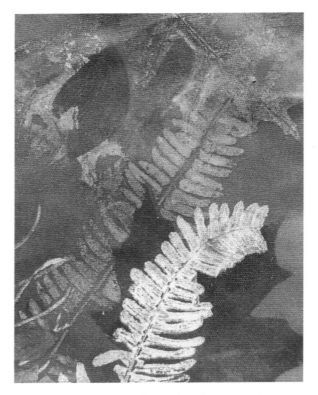

Detail of a canvas bag printed on a walking press.

GOOD TO KNOW

Troubleshooting your prints

• *My print is faint.* Add more ink to your palette and to your brayer. It may also help to add a dime sized amount of ink extender to the ink before you roll it out again.

You can print a new, darker leaf over the first and no one will be the wiser.

• *My leaves printed in one big blob!* When you print leaves in an overlapping pattern, make sure that each leaf is a different color.

If you do end up with a blob, fixing it is easy. Simply reprint part of the pattern *using the same leaves* but selecting different colors, possibly mixing opaque white into your ink colors. This will make the new print opaque and it will cover the old one. Make the new print by aligning the leaf (with its new color) exactly over the old, unwanted print. Cover the leaf with newsprint, rub, and lift to reveal your fix.

CHAPTER 13

BUILD A WALKING PRESS OR STOMPING PRESS • CARVE A STAMP

THREE EXTRAS FOR YOUR ART

STARTING

The Walking Press is a family project. With adults or older kids helping, children as **young as 6** can make prints using a walking press. **Kids 12 and up** can assemble the press on their own and may need only a bit of adult help to gather the supplies.

The Stomping Press variation is great for **kids 4 and up**

Carving Stamps in erasers works for **kids 10 and up**

BEST IN

Any season to put the press together or to carve stamps

Spring through fall to make leaf prints

WHERE

Outside in the shade or indoors

TIME

Once you have the supplies, 30 minutes to assemble the walking press or carve a stamp.

A WALKING PRESS USES THE WEIGHT OF YOUR ENTIRE BODY to make a print on fabric or paper. *You are the press* as you walk over fleece blankets and plywood to make a print.

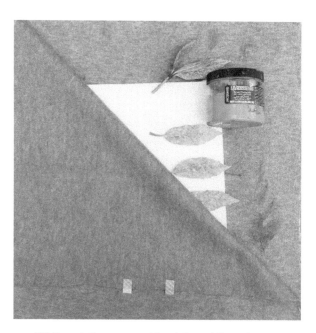

White printing paper, blue ink and three leaves waiting for printing inside the three by three foot walking press. The top blanket of the press is folded over.

During printmaking, the harder you press on your leaf, your wood block, or your rubber stamp, the crisper and clearer your final print. Hand printing, especially onto fabric, may not give you that sharp print, especially if the fabric is a coarse linen or cotton canvas.

Let the walking press step in. You can make it from scrap plywood or drywall from the hardware store and a polar fleece blanket cut to size. The final dimensions are up to what you can find—my two presses measure approximately 3 x 3 feet, and I store them flat in the studio when I'm not printing with them.

BUILD A WALKING PRESS

You need

Plywood or wallboard scrap, cut to approximately 3 x 3 feet. You can use smaller scrap, too, but 3 x 3 will allow you to print a large t-shirt with ease.

A polyester fleece blanket, inexpensive or old. Cut the blanket into two pieces that match the size of the plywood scrap. You need a blanket with some spring in it to cushion your print, so a new fluffy towel would work, but a worn towel or old cotton tablecloth would be too thin.

Double-sided carpet tape

Assemble the press

• **Lay the plywood** or wallboard on the floor.

• **Cut 3 inch pieces of carpet tape** and place it around

the edges of the plywood, spacing it evenly, and rubbing each piece to adhere it firmly. Remove the paper covering the top surface of the tape.

• **Cover the tape** with one layer of fleece blanket, lining it up with the edges of the plywood. Press down firmly to adhere the blanket to the carpet tape.

• **Choose one edge of the plywood** to be the top. Place three or four pieces of carpet tape on the blanket along this top edge. Press down firmly and remove the paper covering the top surface of the tape.

• **Cover the tape** with the second layer of fleece blanket, lining it up with the edges of the plywood and pressing it onto the tape. This second layer is now a flap of blanket attached to the top edge of the press.

Use the press

You will also need a few sheets of newsprint or newspaper to keep the ink off the blankets.

• **Lift the top blanket** and place a sheet of clean newsprint on top of the bottom blanket.

• **Place your printing paper** or cloth on top of the newsprint.

• Arrange inked leaves **ink side down** on top of the paper.

You can use your fingers or tweezers to place the leaves. See **Chapter 10** for more on inking leaves.

• **Place a second sheet** of newsprint on top of the leaves. If the leaves have ink on both sides, you can experiment by placing a sheet of printing paper on top of the leaves instead. You might get a beautiful print off this back side of the leaves.

• **Cover with the top fleece blanket.**

• **With stocking feet,** walk on the blanket, feeling for the shapes of leaves under your feet. Walk over the leaves for about one minute.

• **Lift the top blanket** and remove your print. If the leaves are stuck to the paper, lift them with tweezers to avoid smudges.

GOOD TO KNOW FOR YOUNG CHILDREN: STOMPING PRESS

Old-fashioned telephone books are hard to come by, but they do make great stand-ins for a walking press. In fact, you can use any thick book for this "stomping press" but the book will never be the same after the kids finish making their prints!

Here's how

• **Arrange inked leaves ink side down on top of a sheet of printing or copy paper. T**he paper should be the same size as the book, or smaller, just to make it easy to tuck between the pages of the book. You can use your fingers or tweezers to place the leaves. See **Chapter 10** for more on inking leaves.

• **Open the book to a middle page** and slide in the leaf and paper combination.

• **Close the book and walk** (or stomp!) on the cover for 30 seconds.

• **Open the book,** remove your paper, and lift off the leaf.

CARVE A STAMP

Japanese gyotaku artists sign their prints with a signature stamp called a *hanko.* The hanko refers to the actual characters of a name or it may stand for an animal or phrase. Your family might have a favorite animal or word or holiday that you could select a symbol from to create a similar stamp, it doesn't have to be in Japanese. These stamps, carved from stone in Japan but from erasers in my studio, measure one to two inches high and one inch wide.

Japanese characters for dragon (left) and wisdom (right). In *dragon*, I carved out the background surrounding the character. In *wisdom,* I carved out the characters themselves.

I make my own stamps because I like to carve! But, a one-inch square of small bubble wrap or even a fingerprint can become a stamp by lightly inking the bubble wrap, or a fingertip, and pressing it onto the paper. A local copy store such as Office Depot or an online shop through Etsy or Zazzle can make a rubber stamp out of your idea, too.

You need

Alvin white pencil eraser

<u>OR</u>

Speedball speedy-cut print block

Stamp pads in red and black

Rice paper to test prints

Linoleum cutting tool

X-acto knife, cutting mat and ruler

Let's start

• **Measure a one-inch square** onto the speedy cut print block. If using an eraser, measure your square on the widest flat side.

• **Photocopy a Japanese character** from a dictionary or print it out from the web, sizing it to fit onto your printing block. Choose words that inspire you! "Peace," "good luck," and "wisdom," are some of my favorites. Printmaking reverses lettering as well as your image, so you will be carving the letters in reverse. This may sound confusing, but all you have to do is:

• **Turn the photocopy over** and press the printed side onto the printing block , rubbing hard to transfer the toner from the paper to the block. You will carve these reversed letters, and they will print correctly for reading.

• **When you lift the paper,** you will see the reversed character has transferred to the block. You can carve *around* the character as I did for **dragon,** above, or you can carve your word *into* the stamp as I did for **wisdom.**

• **Using red or black ink,** stamp your print.

Student flounder print, 11 x 14 inches, with hand-carved red "dragon" stamp

ACKNOWLEDGMENTS

MANY THANKS to the master teachers and collaborators who graciously shared their classrooms with me: Kathy Cumberland, Traci Fairbairn, Maggie Kay, Sharon Lundahl, and Lisa Wroblewski.

For the fabulous editor's eyes of Shelly Fierston and Betsy Kulamer and the "hold the course" encouragement of Susannah Figura, Charlotte McNaughton, Lauren Milana, Norman Rosenthal and Annette Ward.

To NPS members Donna F. Allen, John Dougherty, Charlotte Elsner, Gudrun Garkish, Christine Holden, Sharron Huffman, Dwight Hwang, Don Jensen, Lori Loftus, Matt Monahan, Bee Shea, and Nora Terwilliger for their lively professional printmaking advice on worms, fish, fruit, leaves, spiderwebs, and octopi.

To the wonderful Kristin Anderson and Lora Spielman out at Happy Isles, Yosemite National Park, who collect leaves for me and make my way easy in that most beautiful spot.

And of course to Captain Ben Berman and Rose who were there from the start.

SELECTED LINKS AND SOURCES

SELECTED LINKS

Artists and Authors

Edwards, Betty | drawright.com

Gastinger, Lara | laracallgastinger.com/work#/nebel

Goldsworthy, Andy | artnet.com/artists/andy-goldsworthy

Hwang, Dwight | fishingforgyotaku.com

Kim, Byron| nga.gov/collection/art-object-page.142289

Rankin, Laura |

kirkusreviews.com/book-reviews/laura-rankin/the-hand-made-alphabet

To Do

Audubon.org | Excellent resource for building home nature habitats, for sketching in nature, for activities in nature with kids. Click on "Get Outside" from the home page, then "Activities."

Dick Blick art supplies | *dickblick.com* Huge selection of art supplies, shipped worldwide, and there might be a brick and mortar store in your area, too. Discounts often listed at top of website.

eBird | *eBird.org* Identify and record bird sightings whenever you are outside in this citizen science project from the Cornell Lab of Ornithology.

Foldscope paper microscope | *foldscope.com*. Foldscope is a paper microscope that you assemble yourself. After you build your microscope, you can see bacteria, blood cells, and single-celled organisms and close-up views into larger things like insects, fabrics, and fingernails.

GPC Papers | *gpcpapers.com/products/category/thai-unryu* Stop right here to check out beautiful and unusual art papers.

Leaf-id.com | identifies leaves by shape.

National Phenology Network | *usanpn.org* Wonderful worldwide resource for tracking seasonal change in plants and animals. Click on "Volunteer Scientist" to connect with family-friendly Nature's Notebook.

Nature Printing Society |

natureprintingsociety.org Start nature printing and join this friendly international group. Learn how to make prints from nature with one of their expert books, or adults can attend the yearly conference, held in late summer or fall.

PlantNet | *identify.plantnet.org* This free app can identify leaves from your photo.

Project Budburst | *budburst.org* Watch and record the flowering of trees and plants in this citizen science project based at the Chicago Botanic Garden.

Urban Sketchers | *urbansketchers.org* Urban Sketchers is a worldwide network of artists who practice on-location drawing from the windows of their homes, from a cafe, at a park, standing by a street corner... drawn on location, not from photos or memory.

Sketchbook Skool | *sketchbookskool.com* No matter what your age or background, you can make art. These jolly online classes encourage you to make art every day, anywhere.

Zooniverse.org | *zooniverse.org* Help scientists collect data for their research by searching for animals and stars, reading historic diaries, all as part of citizen science.

SELECTED PRINT SOURCES

Fun and practical art instruction

The Art of Printing From Nature: 40th anniversary edition, Nature Printing Society (Nature Printing Society, 2016)

Color, Betty Edwards (Putnam, 2004)

Creating Art From Nature: How to handprint botanicals John Doughty and Sonja Larsen (Doughty and Larsen, 2008)

Drawing on the Right Side of the Brain, Betty Edwards (Putnam, 1989)

An Illustrated Journey: Inspiration from the private art journals of traveling artists, illustrators and designers, Danny Gregory (HOW Books, 2013)

<u>*Kids and nature*</u>

Childhood and Nature: Design principles for educators, David Sobel (Stenhouse Publishers, 2008)

One Small Square: Backyard, Donald Silver (McGraw Hill Education, 1997)

Sharing Nature With Children, Joseph Cornell (Dawn Publications, 1998)

Theater Games for the Classroom, Viola Spolin (Northwestern University Press, 1986)

Watershed: A successful voyage into integrative learning, Mark Springer (National Middle School Association, 1994)

<u>*Fish, trees and birds*</u>

Micronesian Reef Fishes: A field guide for divers and aquarists, Robert F. Meyers (Coral Graphics, 1999)

Reading the Forested Landscape: A natural history of New England, Tom Wessels (Countryman Press, 1997)

The Singing Life of Birds, Donald Kroodsma (Houghton Mifflin, 2005)

<u>*Out in the forest*</u>

Forest Bathing: How Trees Can Help You Find Health and Happiness, Li Qing (Viking, 2018)

My First Summer in the Sierra, John Muir (Houghton Mifflin Company, 1911)

Obata's Yosemite: The letters of Chiura Obata from his trip to the High Sierra in 1927, Yosemite Association (Yosemite Association Press 1993)

Time, Andy Goldsworthy (Abrams, 2000)

INDEX

ABOUT THE AUTHOR

Sue Fierston's art studio is just outside Washington, D.C.

 She leads classes in *gyotaku*, the Japanese art of fish printing, in the studio arts program at the Smithsonian and is an artist-in-residence at Yosemite National Park. For over 15 years she has been a teaching artist, collaborating with teachers to bring the fine arts into schools.

She grew up in the Marshall Islands, 2,500 miles southwest of Hawaii, wading with tropical fish on the reef at low tide.

For more books and updates
Swinging Bridge Press
Instagram • @Suefierston